wendy anderson

The Jesus Experience
Published by Wendy Anderson
New Zealand

© 2014 Wendy Anderson

ISBN 978-0-473-29532-5 (Softcover)
ISBN 978-0-473-29533-2 (ePUB)
ISBN 978-0-473-29534-9 (Kindle)

Production & Typesetting:
Andrew Killick
Castle Publishing Services
www.castlepublishing.co.nz

Cover design:
Paul Smith

Scriptures marked RSV are taken from
the Revised Standard Version of the Bible,
copyright 1946, 1952 and 1971
the Division of Christian Education of
the National Council of Churches of Christ in the USA.
Used by permission. All rights reserved.

Scriptures marked TLB are taken from
the Living Bible
copyright 1971 by Kenneth N. Taylor, published 1971.
Copyright used by permission of Tyndale House Publishers, INC.
All rights reserved.

Scripture quotations marked (NIV) are taken from the
Holy Bible, New International Version®, NIV®.
Copyright © 1973, 1978, 1984 by Biblica, Inc.™
Used by permission of Zondervan. All rights reserved worldwide.

ALL RIGHTS RESERVED

No part of this publication may be reproduced,
stored in a retrieval system, or transmitted
in any form or by any means, electronic, mechanical,
photocopying, recording or otherwise,
without prior written permission from the author.

# acknowledgments

I wish to thank the people who have helped me to complete this book: my husband John, my brother Denny, my mother and some dear friends. Their encouragement and support have been marvellous. I also very much appreciate the services of First Editing and editor David in fixing and polishing my story. Again thank you to Andrew of Castle Publishing for all his professional work and skills.

Thank you all for the prayer; much needed and most gratefully received.

*Wendy*

If you would like to make contact for any reason, please email us:

Wendy's email address: wendys.jesus@gmail.com
Denny's email address: dennisdwyer@clear.net.nz

# contents

| | |
|---|---|
| Chapter 1 | 9 |
| Chapter 2 | 15 |
| Chapter 3 | 21 |
| Chapter 4 | 25 |
| Chapter 5 | 37 |
| Chapter 6 | 39 |
| Chapter 7 | 43 |
| Chapter 8 | 47 |
| Chapter 9 | 55 |
| Chapter 10 | 61 |
| Chapter 11 | 67 |
| Chapter 12 | 75 |
| Chapter 13 | 83 |
| Chapter 14 | 91 |
| Chapter 15 | 97 |

# Chapter 1

*Each time he said, "No. But I am with you; that is all you need. My power shows up best in weak people." Now I am glad to boast about how weak I am; I am glad to be a living demonstration of Christ's power, instead of showing off my own power and abilities. Since I know it is all for Christ's good, I am quite happy about "the thorn," and about insults and hardships, persecutions and difficulties; for when I am weak, then I am strong – the less I have, the more I depend on him. 2 Corinthians 12:9,10 (TLB)*

Hi, pull up a chair and make yourself comfy. Indulge yourselves laugh, cry, yell and smile: join us in life's adventures, guided by my brother Denny and I (Wendy)! We are putting ourselves out there…

Please be ready for anything to happen. Are you feeling brave enough for a roller coaster ride? I know that Jesus is in the seat beside me as he is encouraging the ride of this story.

Do you remember Batman and Robin, those defenders of good against evil? Well think of me as Batwoman as you read this, except she is large and incapable of acrobatics. (Sorry real Batman, but it is a compliment).

Though I am an ordinary woman (despite also being

Batwoman), I and my brother have led extraordinary spiritual lives, all courtesy of Jesus and the Holy Spirit and our choice to follow Jesus, to the very depth of our souls. Not many choose to go all the way with Jesus and consequently, they miss out on so much. I confess; I have a way to go yet. We also pray and trust Father God to do his part of supplying the increase, popularity, purpose for this book, in Jesus' name. We trust him to bring whoever he wants to read this story and to do with it as he wishes.

Here is how it starts. I have known Jesus for 40 years and my brother has know Him for 15. We are the middle siblings in our family. No we are not yet long in the tooth, just getting there. We are in our fifties.

I met Jesus for the first time when I was 15 years old. At the time, I had left home, a small country town close to my grandparents' farm, to work in the city of Auckland. I went to board with an ex-Exclusive Brethren family who took in boarders. I felt safe there with these people. They asked me to go along with them to an Assemblies of God (AOG) church and here was where I met Jesus and asked forgiveness for my sins and became a child of God. I had been to the church a few times and had learnt that, just going to church wasn't enough, but that you had to invite Jesus personally into your life and I noticed a growing conviction to do just that!

I made the decision to take Jesus at his word, because I wanted to and I felt this compelling, insistent need to; which I understand was the Holy Spirit drawing me to Jesus, I was aware of His presence and I could not have ignored Him even if I had wanted to, which I did not. I could feel the presence of Jesus filling the missing void in me.

*Chapter One*

Jesus isn't pushy, he gives us a choice as to whether we will have Him in our lives or not. I had attended Presbyterian Sunday school as a kid but I hadn't known this until I went to the AOG church, where I gained much more spiritual knowledge which would only grow in the years to come.

I remember in one service the person sitting next to me said, "Wow you were really in the Lord there," meaning I was wrapped up in the Lord, so to speak.

I was only aware of His presence and nothing else around me penetrated through His presence. The Lord was ministering just to me alone; it was private.

I replied, "Something left me!"

"Oh, don't tell anybody else that!"

"What?" I said in my ignorance as a fairly new Christian. Basically Jesus had delivered me of a demon that had been in me, which I had had no clue of up unto then!

And if you are wondering, as it was a Pentecostal Church, did they speak in gobbley gook language? (My brother's name for the Holy Spirit's language, the story is in the book of Acts chapter 2.) The answer is yes!

One time, at another service, while I was listening to the sermon, tears just started rolling down my face and they didn't stop for quite a while. The Holy Spirit was upon me, ministering to me. What I can tell you of then, was that I was healed from the hurts that had originated from my own natural father. Some nice kind women came and sat by me and chatted to me and took me to counselling.

The best way to try and explain the hurts I refer to here is to reveal what my father was like; all bitter, cruel, not happy, and lost in himself. (A grizzly bear in a bad mood and like a platted loaf of bread at the same time – twisted.) He was a big man and the rages/tantrums were scary. We were emotionally abused, threatened and scared witless. There were a few hidings. We were unloved and dragged up. None of the extended family liked father, so we were not welcome. I did not have one friend. I remember fighting for survival on all levels. We were alone. There were four of us children, two other sisters and my brother. We were all products of our environment, Mother did her best. We were told on a fairly regular basis that we were not wanted – crushing beyond belief!

In those days, I would enjoy walking up to the Baptist Tabernacle Book Shop to buy Christian music and a Bible dictionary, an exciting thing for a girl out there by herself managing on a small wage, and I still have that dictionary today! The family I lived with gave me my first King James Bible, which I treasure for two reasons: it is the Lord's word, and it was a cherished gift. I just love how the words just jump out at me when the Holy Spirit is communicating to me, so that I can grow to be like Jesus as the Father instructs. This is what it has been like right from the start of accepting Jesus into my heart and life and choosing to serve Jesus himself as my King, who now sits on the right hand side of the Father. Jesus acts as our high priest, replacing the priests and sacrifices of Old Testament times.

It was also during this time that I met my first real Christian friend, another boarder with whom I shared a room. Her friendship was fantastic and going to her family up North meant a lot to me and also taught me a lot. They added more input, character stuff, family relationships, teaching life skills and most of all being welcome and included, all these things and more, enriched me as a person; like building blocks, that my grandparents had started, so that I would become a well rounded adult and a worthwhile member of society. My grandparents had been my saving grace, the only solid base I had had till they died; so having my friends family experience on top of that; was just "what the doctor ordered." It was great medicine. I believe Jesus gave me this experience of my friends family, so I would know what a decent loving family was; part of the healing process to help me from which I not only learned a lot but which kept me grounded and encouraged to persevere in life. I was never a bad girl, but I did lack a few social graces, and was sometimes a bit ignorant, or just plain naive, which is generally sneered at! I don't think my friend or her family ever realized just what they had done for me. They must not know I've missed them terribly, but at least I had that time with them and I am grateful and appreciative; thank you, Jesus.

(Now, Batwoman goes forward and is joined by Robin, my brother, of course!)

# Chapter 2

Dear, Dear Brother, I really wanted to say thanks for being my dear brother. Indeed, you have been a blessing to both John and I. As I think about the things we were talking about, again I find myself in tears, but there is joy in my heart as well just to have your company again. And I am so excited that you too also know Jesus. That's just terrific. To hear of your spiritual experiences in the Spirit is marvellous – to be able to share and pray, even better!

But I want to tell you that despite the challenges of our upbringing, you have turned out a fine man, a difficult feat for someone who grows up without a decent role model. I am sorry I did not realize that you felt so alone, left by yourself. I guess when you are young; there is a lot you do not know. But I do know it was a matter of survival. The only relief was at Nana's and Grandpop's, on the farm, while they were alive. Mother must have found it harder, after they died.

I would like to be able to help you in your present difficulties, but *how* is the question. Definitely prayer support; I have your back covered bro. Let me know too if there is any practical things that John and I can help you with, please dear Bro. Hearing the anguish in your voice, tears me apart. Your story has become like Job's, but remember that Job was blessed in the latter part of his life. Please Lord, may it be the same for my dear brother, and all the harm Satan has caused will be turned to good, In Jesus' Name Amen.

You have been crushed, but you are not dead, the Lord God is looking out for you and is in control of everything. You are in fact a walking miracle, a testimony to the Lord's Glory, His might, his grace, his love, his care. If that is not a privilege, then I don't know what is!

We are still both alive. One day the Father will come for us all. In the meantime, we must do as He leads us. It may not be easy, but be guided by His Spirit, bro. Let Jesus give you strength.

An image came to mind the other day. I was on a swing, which I adore still at my age, basking in the fresh air, outside, the freedom, and with a smile I thought *I am swinging towards Heaven and then back to earth*. It's a lovely picture of pure happiness. But I haven't a clue as to what it means! Maybe you do.

There is joy for you too. You are not alone anymore. And the Father (Dad) has always been there for you too; in fact He has carried you and the depth of your relationship with Dad (The Lord God). This privilege has given you so much; richness, insight, prophecy, depth, spiritual visits/journeys, out of this world stuff and more. Not many go there! So hopefully what I am trying to say; is that out of trauma is a jewel. How does it feel bro to be a jewel? I can see a pair of legs with boots on, shaking off the muck from his boots and a man walking on his way, free of the muck. Bro, is this the Holy Spirit telling you something?

We stand strong when we stand together.

John did give me a different life, from what I could have

had. Yes, he is marvellous, but he hasn't always been there for me, not deliberately, just that he found it difficult to deal with his family as he was hoping they would change, even though he felt they would not and his family made life hell for me (for us) and tried all the time to break us up (but we are a team, committed). Their hostile attitudes persist, and John has put a stop to their influence only by cutting off ties with them, which I would have liked to have done a long time ago! They even tried to destroy the kids, even now, when they are adults, telling them they would split us up, claiming 'your mother is bad,' etc. They were Masonic Lodge people, in the higher realms of that society, which is anything but Christian, making life difficult for us; necessitating intercession to break the satanic bonds. John's parents were doing their best to turn John away from the Father and or stunt his growth in the Lord. All this stuff caused no end of trouble and unpleasantness; Satan does not give up easily. I thought when I married John, I would have a nice family, but I was wrong! As a result of their machinations, I am, unfortunately, very familiar now with manipulation, vindictiveness, deceit, and spite.

I pray that John will be closer to the Lord too, so that we are totally on the same page, so to speak, in all biblical truths. John is a great guy, as you know, with working together that week on the bathroom renovation. I just could be biased, for sure. We were and still are appreciative of your help. It was the first real Christian help bro we have had in decades; sad but true! Thanks again. I'm so glad Dad (the Father) told you to come, not only for your help and witness but for yourself alone too and to share our lives and we will stick together and that is a promise. I do not do and say things lightly, but when

I do, I mean them (a rare quality these days, I know.) I will stand up and fight without a moment's hesitation. That's what a spiritual warrior is meant to do. *A dog with a bone! Never give up when it's the right thing to do or the Lord is saying so!*

Well, we have certainly endured our battles, and learned from them. We wouldn't be what we are if we weren't forced to deal with these conflicts head on. Satan never wins in the end! Got to keep up the fighting, the goal is in sight and we can't lose it. Weariness is one of Satan's tactics, and we cannot succumb. The battles are long and hard but victory is ours if we persevere.

"The battle is long, don't lose victory by fainting." (unknown)

Genesis 41:52 "FOR God hath made me (Denny) fruitful in the land of my affliction."

It is marvellous, bro, that you have been blessed with a lovely wife and now a gorgeous little girl. And another job that you can manage physically, despite the injuries sustained from building all those years. Dad is watching over you through it all; thank you Dad.

While I think about it bro, would you please pray for me? My clot leg from the knee down is daily turning a shade of light purple due to the lack of circulation. It niggles away there in the back of my mind from time to time, I normally take no notice, but some prayer support would be deeply appreciated. One more thing too please: I am fighting hard to stay out of a wheelchair, which I will only accept if it is Dad's will; otherwise, onward to victory in Jesus. Dad is looking after me; if he were not I would be dead. Thank you for saying you didn't want to lose me, I am here as long as Dad says so. I am doing all I can to help myself and I don't want hubby feeling lost. It is great to be loved. Just remember bro we love you too and best of all, Dad loves us all. I am constantly aware that it is not my will, but His that matters, to walk closer to Him, and that is what truly dying to one's self means spiritually.

Anyway, dear bro, I thought I would continue on with the rest of story since I know you will enjoy reading it while you recover from your operation. I know you don't mind my doing that since Jesus wants the story shared.

Listen for the trumpet blast announcing the beginning… *wow!*

# Chapter 3

From what my brother tells me, it was the same for him: he also came across another family that he gained much from. He was 12 when I left home and I did not realize how bad things got for him. I was very upset and saddened when I found out only recently that he also had had to stand up to our father, just as I had to. He was hungry all the time, especially after the grandparents died. He said he would walk with Mother to see if there was any food they could afford, but frequently returned home with no groceries. Even today, this story brings me to tears. I am so thankful my brother now knows Jesus. Though things have been rough for him, he has gained much through these experiences.

I never expected to have a Christian brother, which is marvellous! As time has gone on, we are helping each other in the Lord Jesus. We have been given words/messages for each other, being able to pray for each other and being called to intercede for each other. Denny tells me the various messages the Lord has given me for him have been spot on; really, I say, what a surprise... after all brother Jesus gave them to me for you. The messages have been of an encouraging nature in faith mostly with a bit of guidance including answers to specific prayers, some questions relating to this story, even teaching on different biblical subjects along with numerous scriptures.

"Wendy, it is hard at the moment," he says. Yeah I know, at times it is; Satan is firing niggling darts at you, we'll pray for the Lord's help and bind Satan, is that ok? "Yeah and Jesus does tell us that 'the way is very narrow', but it's so worth it; life changing and having a sovereign God for a Dad and a brother in Jesus and a friend in the Holy Spirit." Remember all the things you have to thank Dad for, all the answered prayers for a start.

And then there is a role change, 'the boot on the other foot' and Denny becomes the teacher and his stories are faith-building material; like going spiritual flying with Jesus; as are the messages Dad has given to him for me. I have just read a true story by Anne Elmer *Transported by the Lion of Judah* it is about her flying trips with Jesus from her hospital bed! Jesus takes her on His back in the image of the Lion, being Himself, to visit different churches round the world.

The Sermon on the Mount, in the book of Matthew, chapter 5, is morale-lifting bro, and I have the feeling there is more spiritually to be revealed there! But do trust Father (Dad) no matter what, and do what He tells you to. Ignore me if I contradict what the Father is telling you to do. We will pray that He will carry you as He promises and that all the evil that has been trying to harm you, bro, will be turned to good.

There is another story my brother related to me that I would like to share with you, another tearjerker. After I had left home, our father shifted the family to Albany, three hours north of Tuakau over the Auckland Harbour bridge, to what then was all farming country for Mother to run a café. There

*Chapter Three*

was on-site accommodation along with it and of course he insisted it was going to be a real goldmine – the usual talk, except he did not expect to work too. So my brother saved up real hard to get his bus fare in order to be able to go and visit with his friend back in Tuakau, a long trip requiring three different buses. He had a great time and was given lunch too, which he ate with relish, he told me, as he had never seen so much food to eat in one place! He could eat whatever and as much as he wanted; a welcome change from being hungry all the time.

He was so happy to be given lunch and that day he was not hungry. I was so moved and grateful for this occasion that he had been given this treat, though it saddens me to think of the hunger and neglect he endured in his youth. I know it still means a hang of a lot to him. He was stunned when the father of his friend said he would run him home again, as it was a long way, three hours one way, and he still had his return bus fare in his pocket. We were not used to this sort of care and our own father would demand the little savings from our school bank books. We both had had to hand over the money or face traumatic consequences. Talk about robbing children.

My brother has been given the privilege of spiritual journeys in the line of the Peretti books, a series of novels about spiritual warfare. I sent my brother "The Prophet" book early on, which enlightened him to what was going on with him. Wasn't his sister generous with her precious few books!

# Chapter 4

My doctor's consulting room feels like a gentlemen's library in an old house, as the doc's books line a wall. Indeed it is a room in an old house, on a normal domestic family section in the suburbs: green grass and trees and shrubs at the front and down the side of the driveway. The room itself is cast in shadow today, producing a dimness which is strangely comforting.

This is where my husband and I were before heading south for a family event. We had made time for the doctor's visit as we lived four hours away, and took the opportunity before continuing our journey. As an afterthought, I asked the Doc what was this lump on my leg?

"Let's look," he said. "Wendy, you have a melanoma and it needs to come off, now."

"Oh," I said in total ignorance! "After our visit down south please," I said, thinking *I don't like this!* Needles! Quick run!

The doc frowned and told me to book an appointment on my way out.

Back in his rooms a few weeks later, after crossing the Southern Alps again, in winter, like an arduous game of ping pong. Or like an Australian boomerang, thrown in one direction only to be pulled back in the opposite one.

*The Jesus Experience*

"Hop up onto that bed," the doctor said. "You'll only feel a scratch."

Yeah. Okay? Panic! Feeling somewhat anxious would be an understatement! Needles! I close my eyes and don't look! The word wimp comes to mind, not at all comforting! Gibbering idiot definitely fits the bill. Then, the doc informs me there's another mole he doesn't like the looks of and its coming off too. *Great...*

So he proceeded to perform the little surgery and then informs me they have to go to the lab and that he'd be in touch. Wonderful, *not!*

We go home again, just a wee bit down the road! (The trip is actually across the width of the country, coast to coast, west to east, through the Alps.) We traversed the Southern Alps, yet again, back to the doc's, just like reliable homing pigeons.

Now Wendy, he began, the result says you have a malignant melanoma and you need further surgery by a cosmetic surgeon. This time, he'll have to remove a very large area. You will receive an appointment shortly.

Home again James! Back through the snow and ice, Porters Pass to climb and the zigzag to descend. We don't normally travel this route in winter, as it is a tricky road at the best of times. But we did not have a doctor on the West Coast at that time, as none of them were taking on new patients, so we were not the only ones traversing the Southern Alps for a doctor! In fact, several times we had to travel through the alps for afterhours surgery, so it was not a new experience.

It is a three and a half hour journey to the edge of the city. In the days before the new Viaduct, we had to put our head lights on full and foot down in order to climb the steep Otira Gorge.

In addition, you had to cope with drivers unfamiliar with the highway, who had no idea just how tricky the road was to navigate, unaware of the huge drops, and missing seeing a prominent sign saying "give way to uphill traffic!" Out of necessity we used to use the air horns as a safety measure. Also in earlier days, some creeks hadn't been bridged yet, and there are still numerous one-lane bridges today. You are quite literally enclosed, encircled, with mountains towering over you and at their mercy, as you are in the "High Country," meaning mountain conditions.

Uphill, on the coast side, lies a section of the road that was one-way for a bit, with a waterfall trickling over the road. At the top of the zigzag on the return journey, the road, narrows drastically and is also falling away, then it disappears into space, so to speak, and it is quite freaky to the uninitiated after skirting across a gravel slope coming down. The zigzag was not a series of straight stretches with a bend at the end of them, but rather a series of tight, bends or half circles and full circles. It was tenuous to say the least! An aerial photo of this sends shivers down the spine while praying "Please be merciful oh God!"

The first time that I drove this highway road by myself, some years before, I had difficulty keeping the car stationery, while waiting for the uphill traffic on the one way section of the gorge road; before I could continue on down the gorge; it was like trying to keep a missile (car) in control. Consequently, on the way home again I pulled over at the bottom of the gorge to let a Morris 1300 pass me, as I was scared about getting back up the steep incline. I did not know how the tyres managed to stick to the road; it always felt like you were about to fall off the road! In those days, we had a very old XJ6 Daimler, that weighed a ton and had a powerful engine, and it was this car that day I was driving! And I let a small Morris 1300 pass me so I could crawl up the gorge.

As you can imagine when, trembling with fear, I finally told my husband of my actions, I got the typical bloke's reaction: he shrieked at me as his eyebrows climbed through the skyline. It is especially worse when they are car buffs; at one time, hubby even had to teach a racing driver how to drive bends. So I was not popular at that moment!

Today this alpine pass is equally tricky, but the zig-zag has been replaced with a viaduct and there are two lanes in the gorge, now.

Meanwhile, back east again, feeling like a ping pong ball. This time it was the cosmetic surgeon's chair I was sitting in, waiting for the needles to begin! A very different kettle of fish, this is now. At least his waiting room had a calming effect, briefly, surrounded by windows allowing one to enjoy the flowers and trees from the wrap-around garden while admiring the nice furniture and fancy, intellectual magazines! I figured I was paying for that too, so might as well enjoy it! Mind you the surgeon seemed ok; at least I hoped so as my doctor had recommended him! *Such generosity, eh!* (He was!)

Unfortunately, his impressive surgery did not have the same calming effect on me; as his waiting room had. The surgeon looked and sounded like he knew his trade, "the genuine article," so I should have taken confidence in that, had I even thought of it! I don't remember praying either; I was "too wound up like a corkscrew" to think! It was all over in about half an hour and a very deep 10 centimetre radius

*Chapter Four*

had been taken out. Everything, he said, had been removed. That, I guess was my birthday present, to be appreciated later, when the penny dropped! (No cancer had been found in the bloodstream.)

We stayed overnight out of necessity. It was a funny birthday; instead of the usual festive activities, I got someone digging round in my leg, as my fun for the day, getting paid to sharpen their knife wielding skills!!

It was all downhill after that, and that did not include the trip home. Hindsight is a wonderful thing, they say. It is just as well we did not know what was about to happen, I think? *Forewarned is forearmed?* Sometimes! Thank goodness the Lord does and I am confident in him. I still do not know today, ten years later, what is his purpose in all this and may never know. I just keep on trusting Him as we are told to do.

But before I proceed, allow me to introduce myself first. My name is Wendy and my husband of 37 years is John. Thirty-seven years! Indeed time flies (or speeds away like a runaway train!) But we are not old yet! We have two adult children, two grandchildren and we live on the West Coast; being the rain forest region of the South Island New Zealand.

As for myself, I am terribly attractive, simply gorgeous! (Yeah, right!) I am still blonde but highly intelligent, I hope. Nice, kind, a good heart, always smiling, positive, a real character, direct (don't ask unless you want an honest answer), funny, creative and a spiritual warrior, willing to go out on a limb with extreme curves now, prone to wearing glasses and dangling earrings, bright coloured clothing, and don't forget the lippy (lipstick), artist, business type, wife (with a sometimes adoring husband). Oh, I nearly forgot, driving hubby mad with my witty comebacks is good fun! He has taught me well! His facial expression often seems to say "What now?" Dear man! One can't be dull, eh? Where's the fun in that?

Hubby is *lovely* but slim like a bean pole. (That's not fair!) His brown hair is only just starting to go grey, lucky beggar, but he does have a solar panel on the top of his head! He is tall, wears glasses, has a great *dry* sense of humour and is part Scottish. Would you believe a pretend Laird? He is a fine husband, devoted father, skilled accountant, and fantastic musician. I have told him he is irreplaceable. That might have been a *mistake!*

We usually agree about most things, though we express our agreement in different words, and the disagreements are like two billy goats bucking their heads together, for world domination! Occasionally compromise is necessary. Regardless, we experience much laughter, fun and we work together very well. Life is not perfect; but it is made better by sharing in the ups and downs. We have had a lot of challenges, that's for sure, mostly involving family, but then who hasn't, and we'd be the poorer without them.

We enjoy walking, four-wheel driving, reading, home activities, volunteering, theatre and music. I keep the house and garden going, while I enjoy painting sewing, politics, fundraising, cricket, cycling, swings, fishing and swimming, etc. Unfortunately, physical difficulties have curtailed some of these activities recently. But I do intend to have a version of paddle boarding soon! We also enjoy watching car rallies, exploring, history, and train riding. For our 25th wedding anniversary, we were timing crew in the week-long "Targa Rally" event, for a change.

## Chapter Four

We both have enjoyed volunteering for various things. I have mostly been involved in fundraising, corporate sponsorship and governance. With John, it is music, Red Cross rescue, fire brigade, ambulance. NZ runs on volunteers!

We are just ordinary folk just like others wrapped up in everyday life, coming up to the surface to breathe occasionally!

I have to confess I am prone to putting my foot in it! Have you heard the saying? Well I would say, both feet actually, a bit like falling into a swamp or bog, not a pretty picture. I recall the story of one development project which lost an entire bulldozer this way! My point is that it's easy to sink in over your head, and of course I might add hubby is "full of it" too! Swamp mentality!

Anyway, the story that stands out in my mind the most was the row boat trip up the mighty Waikato River to the whitebait stand on the river. I was around 8 years old, rowing from the local Maori Pa, while Grandpop dealt with the Pa's whitebait for sale. It was a terrifying journey: the river was flowing rapidly, swirling and riding high. My friend and I caught a cup full of whitebait and I refused to go back in the boat, walking back was on the agenda, except it was through a swamp jumping from one clump to the next, avoiding the water, while hearing those dreadful sucking sounds. It was as scary as the river had been! Both places had I fallen in; there was no coming out!

My snow white hair wasn't that colour by the time I got back to the Maori Pa and Grandpop, covered in swamp muck samples for free. Swamps! I haven't been through anymore, just skirt round them instead in the four wheel drive on a road for preference!

Where hubby and I live on the West Coast, you just don't pull off the road anywhere; for example, the main highway running down the Coast is flanked by sea, swamp, bush, lakes, and extremely wet soft ground, more so after heavy rain and it does catch some people out; their vehicles sinking into the ground where they pulled over to stop on the side of the road! On one of our trips down the Coast we came across a motor home tilting on its side, just about to go right over and luckily a beer tanker came up the road and just happened to have a chain to pull them out. Now we have a winch on our vehicle and it has since been used for rescue a few times! Logistics for rescue vary depending on, what it is and where it is. The actual area of the West Coast is a narrow strip of land about 800km in length, chock full of native forest, bush, flax with creeks, rivers, lakes, farmlands, swamps, hills, in between the Southern Alps and the Tasman Sea; till it runs smack bang into the Fiordland World Heritage Park further down the coast line. The "Coast Road," glaciers and the pancakes rocks being star attractions. In paradise there is always a serpent and that is a tiny, tiny, blood sucking insect, in this case, the sandfly which even the locals watch out for them. The West Coast Region is sparsely populated, 30,000 people approximately; the major population concentration being located around the Greymouth District.

The West Coast, however, is a fascinating part of the world, with its heritage and natural wonders and resources. It is a wild pristine region that has "changed little since the dawn of time" possibly; the filming crews seem to think so (natural history unit) if that is anything to go by but Fiordland hasn't changed! If you are a Bear Grylls fan, he has been to New

## Chapter Four

Zealand a few times now filming his survival shows including crossing the Southern Alps to the West Coast; it looked frightening watching it on TV, quite perilous, cliff hanger stuff. Also if you watch "The World's Greatest Motorcycle Rides," you again will see the Coast on TV with him raving about his time in NZ.

Nearby to us is Lake Brunner, a bit of a playground to us. So please join us sitting outside the Station House cafe overlooking the railway line that goes east, "The Trans Alpine" train trip route. Lake Brunner's sparkling blue waters before us and the mountains in the background (Southern Alps) a real light crystal, shimmering blue sky, all sunny and bright clean fresh air you can sniff and taste with a light fairy's wind whispering by and encircling you while joyfully dancing hijinks. The cafe is a picturesque old brown wooden house with picture windows and decking round three sides, with brown wooden tables and chairs and umbrellas outside, in the style of a Cape Cod shorefront house. It is quite a drop down onto the rail lines and the railway station. Just below the station is the local yacht club.

There are willows, pine and native trees fringing most of the lake and a small number of holiday houses. There are recreational boats on the water, skiers too. It is a tiny town in the middle of native trees and countryside thick with brush and vegetation. There is a small convenience shop in the petrol station, a single hotel and a tiny school serving the surrounding farming district. There is a handful of locals living here all year round, but the population swells drastically in the holidays when the holiday homes fill up. You will see pukekos and wekas (NZ native large birds) wandering around as well as farm animals further away from the lake. We have spent a lot of time here beside the lake, an excellent way to blow the cobwebs away. Friends of ours have a holiday house here, so we have been truly blessed with the use of it. There is fishing here and walking too. We enjoy standing on the railway over bridge to watch the train go under our feet while counting today's carriages, in effect becoming a part of the idyllic landscape.

Our house is in a small mining town, up a hillock, at the start of the Coal Creek Falls track. We have a view of The Apostle hills in front of us and to the back, are Mt Searle, Mt Davy and Spring Creek. We get wekas wandering around the backyard and we have to protect the vege garden from them! We have bush and cabbage trees (giant scented lilies) out the back as well with all sorts of bird life, like bell birds and the wood pigeons we call helicopters, named for the sound they make while flying. Then there is the cheeky tui which mimics the bell bird, which has as a fantastic rich high sounding song, to name but a few of them. I have a sort of studio at the back of the garage where I paint my oil paintings and hubby makes do with a spare bedroom for his numerous pianos. If you stand in the middle of the road, or from the walking track where there's a small gap through the bush that offers a glimpse of the sea with its various moods. There are no houses behind us or across the valley.

As the West Coast is a rainforest, we get a lot of rain, so much so that it's measured in metres here. NO KIDDING THERE! Where we are, close to the coast, about four minutes by car, on "the Coast Rd" to Westport we get about two metres a year; and the precipitation only increases further inland. In the Southern Alps it's 8 metres; I believe in Fiordland, way down the West Coast, gets 12 metres annually. We also have some spectacular thunder and lightning storms. But believe it or not we do actually do well for sun too. As I type this, we're being pelted by a sudden, sizeable explosion of hailstones.

The Grey River on the way to town does flow over its banks here and there and cuts us off from Greymouth, the main commercial town on the West Coast about 10 km from us. NZ is built for this. Despite the fabulous scenery, the sparse population and vulnerable mountain passes (which do get cut off fairly often in winter) keep us isolated, to a degree.

You can enjoy tramping, kayaking, fishing, hunting, boating, cycle trails all on our doorstep. It is also rich in history and offers places to explore like Waiuta and Denniston. Denniston is an old coal mining town situated on a plateau 2000 ft above sea level; some of it is still mined. The incline itself is sometimes called the 8th wonder of the world due to its perpendicular railway incline.

We have explored a lot of the Coast by now. Hubby and I enjoy walking the Rewanui, Ten mile, Point Elizabeth and Truman tracks to name a few. I am particularly fond of the short steep tracks, as I grew up with hills. I particularly liked the steep climbs from when we lived on Banks Peninsula on the East Coast of the South Island. My favourite place for praying is outdoors while walking these local tracks.

Also there is a plentiful supply of four wheel drive roads in both regions, which we are grateful for. Inland from us is a tremendous four wheel drive road, a real hidden treasure chest; starting from "frog pond" corner. Opening the treasure chest springs surprise after surprise; a real good kiwi (NZ) adventure into the unknown, surrounded by dense forest while climbing twisty, steep bends under the canopy of the forest, with huge drops over the sides and navigating seven little, rocky river crossings, with care. We found a delightful river gorge of boulders; with the look of North America, if TV is to be believed. Then we were picking our way through a mud slide blocking the road right on the edge of a significant drop into the river below. The day was a real blessing to both of us. It feels quite liberating in the senses, refreshing to my spirit, peaceful and we enjoy the stops strolling in the sunshine; out in nature created by Dad. (All nature praising Dad; written in the Bible.)

Going back to whitebaiting, the West Coast is renowned for having the best bait in New Zealand, especially the bait from South Westland. We used to refer to it as "white gold" here, but that honour has been given to milk now. We go fishing for it in spring and usually freeze it for later use. Here you have to be very careful not to fish in somebody else's whitebait stand as it does not go down very well and there are all sorts of tales on this subject flying round; just think of "The Wild West" cowboys. We ourselves haven't been white baiting for a while.

We do spend a lot of time at home, with our respective interests. Then all of a sudden we are up and off.

# Chapter 5

We are a mixture of country bumpkin/town folk. When the kids were tiny, and we shifted from the country to the city, we were a right pair of country bumpkins, with little knowledge of urban ways or sophistication.

Our first initiation into city ways was rather scary and went like this: there was a prowler, hubby was out … a sudden rattle of the back door … the blur of a face … yoicks! Immediately, I ran to the phone and rung the police to come and they arrived quickly, with a police dog in tow. They were really big men in big boots and of course they went through the house as well, each one of them tripping on the step that couldn't be seen in the dark, as we were in the middle of a DIY project. No one was found. We even put black string across the driveway to see what would happen!

This brush with danger left us unimpressed with city living at this stage! Nerves shattered! We had recourse to ring the police twice more in a short pace of time! One time, we thought the intruder had entered and was inside the home. We were woken out of a deep sleep and hubby had seen a person's shadow. He began yelling at the top of his voice, 'Ring the police', hoping to scare off whoever it was. Once again I found myself on the phone to the police, who duly came and went through everything. This time they all tripped over the base of the archway we were taking out, despite John warning 'mind the step!' They were duly puzzled and we were embarrassed! But they did their thing and left. Later, John concluded the shadow was just a reflection.

Another time at night, with hubby out, the sound of footsteps outside broke the silence. Suddenly, there was a noise at the backdoor! The policemen came again and looked around and found no one, except a few hedgehogs around the back. Oh horrors, I thought, I feel embarrassed again! Nevertheless, the policemen were very kind and didn't make me feel an idiot even though I was! I was not used to having people wandering round your property unwelcomed! Talk about a couple of country bumpkins coming to town; we were not used to that sort of thing!

In another incident, the police were called in broad daylight when a dubious character ran through our section and over the neighbour's fence! Too much excitement! I think they caught him, fortunately. We had no cause to ring the police again, thank goodness!

Some years later we were able to help the police in a burglary case when we lived in Akaroa. The burglar had stayed in our motels for the night after committing a robbery! We were police witnesses! It was the only time we had checked someone in so late!

# Chapter 6

Going back to the early days of my Christian experience, once the AOG people learned I was out there alone, they embraced me and welcomed me into their community. It was balm for a weary spirit. Suddenly, I had an extended large family. I remember once seeing a picture of a little girl walking, thumb in mouth and holding onto an arm of her dangling teddy bear, looking lost, which is what I had felt like, being out there alone; (feeling like a waif and stray! Obviously Batwoman came later!) But now a part of one big happy family of God with Jesus having lots of brothers and sisters, that's got to be good. I think so and I very much treasure that painting of Jesus with his disciples, because it also represents love and family to me as well as sacrifice beyond human understanding. We do sit round that table with Jesus when we partake of communion, but I look forward to it for real in heaven with everyone. Sitting and chatting with prophets and angels is mind blowing enough but to have Dad and Jesus and the Holy Spirit is beyond words – an idea that dazzles with wonder. Talk about a humbling experience. The whole clan!

As I had received a very good grounding in the Bible, along with some powerful, enlightening, Prophetic teaching at the AOG church; which I have always been most grateful for. I was saddened to learn a decade or so later that the minister had gone off the rails; he was so close to the Father. It is a hard job being a minister and Satan really does goes after them for fodder food. Destroying Father's leaders opens the way to gobble the sheep as easy prey; mayhem rears its head; I have seen just this. It is not what Jesus wants for any of us, for that matter he tells us that in the word! I have felt the burden/impression to lift various ministers/leaders up in prayer; as much as they pray for us. That news sparked my interest, in caring for ministers and their families and also; drawing my attention to this particular spiritual battle arena.

For all of us alike; I find a cuppa and a chat and a meal does wonders, taking note much spiritual enrichment happens this way; even in a cricket match, DIY, car rallies etc; I have found! And that includes the AOG family that I boarded with! It has been most enjoyable seeing Jesus present in all our lives/circumstances. Jesus leaves me in awe and wonder. Praise God. To me these interludes are like a gentle Summer's day rain shower, bringing a new freshness, growth, more sparkle and colour in the grass and the fresh scent of the surrounding environment. Guess what- things do not only happen in church, Jesus is everywhere!

I shifted from their (the AOG ex-Exclusive Family) home to a Christian women's hostel, as it was closer to work. The new accommodation sadly lacked the comfy, convivial family atmosphere. It was here that I remember being really miserable over something. I think it was when I discovered the woman that had been giving me a ride to the young adults group was a lesbian. She had ideas, and I couldn't get out of the car fast enough. I remembered being shocked and upset –

*Chapter Six*

I never saw her again, thank goodness. It was a bit much for someone my age to have come across; and I was alone with no one to turn to. (Today I know, it is the sin of homosexuality that is the problem; not the actual person and Jesus loves them too; just not the sin.)

Jesus came to see me, at this time which was deeply moving. I had been kneeling by my bed crying and praying when Jesus came and comforted me. It was the very first visit of many. That first visit from Jesus kept me going and grounded me in him, assuring me that I was not alone. It placed my feet firmly standing on the rock that is Jesus, my Lord and brother, the corner stone, foundation of the Christian church as in the book of Hebrews, in the Bible. He's real; that is why I will never turn my back on Jesus; it is just one confirmation of many from Him that he is real.

Indeed, there have been periods of what feels like the Sahara Desert and there will be a reason for it. I have spent a lot of my Christian life being out there by myself; again there will be a reason for it; I know, and I am all the stronger for it, even if I don't fully understand why. But Jesus' hand is present in everything – even in writing this book. Though I'm not an experienced writer, He has encouraged and inspired me and Jesus has shared His humour with me too and also He was just being plain funny in His visits to me. Tremendous just does not cover it!

It is amazing what you see when you look back, eh?

At 17, I considered going into nursing, but it didn't work out, so I went back to office work and attended the New Life Church, living in their Bible college hostel. This is where I first spoke in the Holy Spirit language (that gobbley gook language!) I just got on with life as one does. A requirement for living at the Bible College included part time Bible study. I remember trying to write a sermon for class and getting told you had us in the palm of your hand and then you flat lined out and left us up in the air!... I had told them all that the Lord had enlightened me too, about the sermon on the mount, but had missed the punch line so to speak! I remember being mortified and feeling embarrassed and wanting to run a mile away! I did not complete the training. That phrase "being young" again rears its head! I mean having limited experience and only a small amount of wisdom to draw upon. Being young has its limitations, I can testify to that!

I met my husband at that time. He was from a Methodist background and though he didn't know Jesus personally then, he believed. He became a Christian and we then went to the Baptist church of a friend of his who did know Jesus. We got married there and stayed in that church, where we made some really good friends. Those days were just living, nothing remarkable, hard work and devotion to the Father. I surmise we were still growing up, growing together. I have often been told "I want what you have" and I reply "that is Jesus you see in me and it is Jesus you too can have. A bloke on our street said that to me recently, so I gave him my copy of "The Shack;" a story about Mack who "spent an entire weekend with God," in a shack in the American woods; to read and I told him "this is what you see." What he is seeing in me; is Jesus. He read it, he tells me, and gave it back with no further comment!

# Chapter 7

My faith is strong, unwavering and absolute. I am one of those of black and white types, but I have learned that there is grey too over the years. The need to be close to Jesus is very real; the Holy Spirit's voice guides me to Him and His will, which ultimately comes from the Father through Jesus, which you learn as you grow in Jesus. (Batwoman had a lot of learning to do; Robin is still learning... ouch!)

Anybody that knows me knows I stick to the Lord like glue and that's the way it is. I think I amuse some as I expect answers to prayers and also pray for car parks and I have the confidence in my personal relationship with Jesus. I do and say as I am told. There have been a few occasions when I have opened my mouth and the words that came out were not mine but the Holy Spirit, leaving me stunned.

Here's a recent example. Hubby was going to strip wall paper and I hadn't been able to do anything for about a year with knee cartilage problems and I had no intention of offering to help as it would be a pretty dumb thing to do! I am not lazy by nature and was feeling terrible as hubby was trying to do too much; normally I am in boots and all, and we have always worked as a team! So the next thing I knew was that my mouth was open and saying "I'll help you!" What! That's not me! Lord?

My sewing will have to wait, so I duly do what I can, despite the pain in the knees, but hey it must have been necessary, so who am I to complain? I normally push myself too hard given my physical conditions. I had missed doing all those sorts of things anyway and it was a morale booster for hubby. Even though I did not achieve much, it did help finish the job and ease the burden. I thought okay Lord; I am taken by surprise, but I am up for a challenge and I trust you!

I don't get answers to all prayers instantly – some are still in the pipe line, it cannot be the right time yet or the answer is no, so I guess I just wait and trust the Father and that is fine as I am safe in His hands.

I believe in helping others as we are told to do (Batwoman rears her head), and I have always done it, whether it was bake a cake, give an honest opinion, pray, play tennis with a neighbour or look after food for those who need a helping hand. That also means being a Christian in attitude as well as action. Some non-Christians I've encountered have turned Jesus down but were still curious about my faith, asking me if I still believed. One of them has since died and did not know the Lord Jesus, a real shame! These particular folk, you would have enjoyed as much as we did, for the simple reason they were real easy to get on with and they were colourful in every sense of the word: diamonds in the rough!

Hubby was working by this time for a bank and transferred to the West Coast, so we got our first house, a very old one, where the front room was partially rotten and the floor was on a slope, the toilet was an add on at the back of the house on a concrete slab with a tin shack covering it. The section was a hay paddock with a goat supplied! It was here we went

*Chapter Seven*

to a local church after meeting a great guy who asked us along, and there we stayed. We had some great friends there and the minister and his wife were absolutely marvellous: tremendous witnesses of the faith and Jesus and our Father God. They were real and practiced what they preached and were of invaluable help to us. They became my yard stick so to speak, the measure of good character and real Christianity in practice. (We have been quite discouraged, in this since!) It was here that the minister asked the congregation to allow the Holy Spirit to come among us, to take our relationship with Dad to a deeper level. Some people frowned upon this; as a common phrase occurs, it's about me not Jesus. The minister sadly does not preach there anymore. It is ultimately about Jesus reigning in the church and not the Devil! That is a real sad situation for Christians, especially so for Jesus as he is the cornerstone of the church which Dad/God the Father gave Him charge over.

We were there for nearly five marvellous years till hubby was transferred again. We had two children in that time too. As to the house, a kind relation, who unfortunately was not a Christian came and helped John fix the rot and put in a sliding door and another concrete slab! The minister (Colin and Faye) came and helped hubby level the floor his way, which was jump on it... it worked!

It was Faye who looked after our daughter, while I had our son in hospital. Colin and Faye were the salt of the earth types and you could not have better friends or champions, aside from Jesus. Faye was a really vibrant petite woman, full of integrity with charming facial features that hinted at her American Indian heritage; she was just great. Colin was a tall, big man with sandy features, an ex-tradesman turned minister in later life, and really comfortable in himself with a heart of a Lion, undoubtedly committed to the gospel of Jesus Christ and the word of God. We loved their company and our friends there, who were genuine, as it should be. That kind of atmosphere was a far cry from the one, for example, in which my hubby grew up. His family was big on control and manipulation, and their devotion to Jesus was superficial (mere lip service). It is a miracle that either of us, are as we are, all due to The Father watching over us from childhood, as I know I could have easily walked different roads, if it wasn't for the Lord watching over me until I knew him personally for myself.

# Chapter 8

When we left the Coast for Christchurch, I must have been around 23. It was here that I came across a Christian woman's organisation that stood for family and men, opposing the feminist crowd against men and families; that preferred to have test tube babies, girl's only, etc., hard core stuff. I got the group off the ground with the help of a couple of older Christian ladies, who took me under their wings. I did enjoy this role very much, especially the colourful press releases; no kidding! (I like it when the good guys win! Do you?) It was very much a cloak and dagger affair; you either like it or not; it's survival of the fittest. Yee-ha! A gun-slinging duel!

I think my own background in childhood with the experience of that women's group and the early church teachings was my preparation for standing up and fighting on the front line for the Lord – the beginning of being a spiritual warrior. I came across a scripture in the Old Testament, saying, who will stand up for me, fight evil, stand in the gap for Him (Father God). That particular verse just about leapt off the page at me, as if to say "Ring, ring, hello, are you listening to me?" Oh yes! I thought, Wendy, pin back your ears, wake up, smell the coffee and take notice!

The communications kept me going over the years, an

indisputable affirmation that God was real, Jesus was real, the Holy Spirit was real as I knew them personally. And also faith is a matter of believing without evidence, but I did get the privilege of seeing Jesus and experiencing answers to prayer from the Father and seeing Him through Jesus and knowing the Holy Spirit is guiding me.

I began hearing the Holy Spirit speak to me more so in my late 20's. We all listen to the radio tuning in and turning up the volume to suit our hearing. Well it was just like that. I chose to turn up the volume to hear more clearly, at the urging of the Holy Spirit saying "this is the way." And I followed the path so to speak laid out by the Holy Spirit for a closer walk with Jesus. I found myself listening for his voice all the time. It has been very rewarding and challenging. I do what He tells me to do and will continue to do so, regardless of any opposition; there is just no contest to compare with following Jesus.

As a result of this, Satan has attacked me many times, and so I take whatever measures are necessary. Obviously I am doing what the Lord would have me do and Satan does not like it. There has been the odd occasion when I have been a bit down, but not for long, an hour or two, as I know Satan likes to make you ineffective, so he can make hay while the sun shines. And my positive nature keeps me from falling into a downward spiral. I am more likely to get the broom out and sweep the rubbish out! My husband, I think, has become used to my "strange" ways, by now. His eyebrows crawl to the skyline on a regular basis!

The Bible says rejoice, be happy; when you are going through a hard time, it means that there is spiritual progress

*Chapter Eight*

being made and battles being won; and that Satan has not stopped me/you from serving Jesus! In my opinion the pain is worth it, it is a calling, and Jesus suffered much more; willingly! Many miss this opportunity to fight for our Lord, but why? I do not know; perhaps it is the fear of the unknown, the fact that it is discouraged, not taught or would require more than they want.

Actually that is how I have grown in the Lord, by being willing and doing. If I had not, I would have missed out on so much, and to me that is a waste of a priceless present wrapped complete with a gauzy, floating, twirling bow. The present represents the beautiful dance with Jesus and the Holy Spirit and Dad twinkling in my heart, pure poetry in motion weaving together a symphony of symmetry spirits.

Satan, of course, wants to take away that nice present. But He cannot take our salvation away, since we will never turn our backs on Jesus. Then there is someone I knew, a church goer whose belief in God was somewhat dubious. Well, one day years later, I came across her again, so I decided to call by with flowers and was greeted with Satan's sneer on her face! It blew me away, I had not expected that! It certainly had me thinking about how the hang had she ended up like that. She/it shut the door in my face, as if Satan were saying "she's mine now." Horrors I thought, and have prayed since about her. Then, it clicked: she was in a church that Satan had taken possession of and that must have been the result! I had seen a darkness about her that I had noticed in someone else that dabbled in cult stuff, a dark evil presence coming out of them like pus!

That is a spiritual fight waiting to happen and the need

for the covering of the blood of Jesus is very real as well as the need of others in Jesus to wage war together; if that is a battle you are called to take on. As Jesus said to Satan, "get behind" (In Jesus' name); in other words go away, you have no authority here! I have also seen Christians stagnating in their walk in Jesus, having fallen victim to Satan's deceit. So there is a big need for intercession and spiritual warriors. Just this very week the Holy Spirit had me praying/interceding for some folk on the prayer request list of the prayer group I am involved with. The focus was not just their immediate needs but on the bigger picture of these requests; for example the root cause of the problem, not the symptom.

We all have a choice and some people do not want to change. That is their choice to make. We will all answer for our choices someday before Father God. As I remember from science class, for every action, there is an equal and opposite reaction. I have always taken note of that and its application manifests in all facets of life.

Saying and doing these things, does not always make me popular, but better to have done what the Lord tells you to than to miss out on the privilege and honour of being asked. We all have moral responsibilities: to speak up and try to prevent a brother or sister from falling by the wayside, and to share with each other what's happening to us, to be encouraging and caring. Tolerance and patience are virtues. Personally I have found it much easier to listen to Jesus and do as he commands. I act in faith that Jesus will carry me through and his word will come to light. I have spoken up when I have been disturbed with what I have seen; and it has not gone down too well. Unfortunately the truth was not always received with

## Chapter Eight

open arms but with closed hearts. Despite every effort to be nice and polite and here's a thought we worry about offending people, yet in the bible did Jesus ever say please and sorry did I offend you, no He did not He just said put down your nets and follow me. All of us are valuable, loved and wanted by the Lord Jesus himself and the Father too. (God loves us all!)

People sometimes ask, if there is a God, why does he not stop bad things from happening? The reality is that Father God has allowed the Earth to become Satan's domain for a certain time. Satan thinks he's going to beat Father God and looks at all the people he will have with him, convinced in all his haughty arrogance that they will worship him instead of God! That is why God sent Jesus to us, so that by dying upon the cross, he would stamp out Satan's hold over death. Through Jesus we have life; we are saved here on earth and will enjoy eternal life beyond the grave.

Father God cannot tolerate sin of any kind. As Christians, we have the privilege to be able to ask for forgiveness for our sins. We are not to make a habit of sinning or thinking it is okay to do wrong as an excuse to sin some more because we have that gift of forgiveness through Jesus. It bothers me greatly, as I have seen just that, but the best thing I can do is pray for them, and leave the rest in Jesus' hands.

At one stage I had the privilege of a "wee" women's ministry, run by Jesus. Basically a few women were put in front of me, so to speak by the Holy Spirit and I listened, supported, chatted and quietly prayed for them. It did me a world of good too, as at that time I had no women's company in my life, and it was a blessing to help others. It was all very convivial and conducted with lady like decorum indulging in cream cakes

*The Jesus Experience*

and tea, "dressed to the nines, to boot!" Yeah, right! Except it was actually while I was walking down a street or on a track in the bush; usually in unexpected places mostly; dressed as a "Scarecrow;" tatty, old gardening clothes, extremely colourful! Not; like the elegant, poised, perfectly made up "Paris model" being served tea and cakes with fine china! Darn! I will get to play ladies yet!

I was tickled pink when one day a younger woman who lived in the other island called to chat about the Holy Spirit. The only person she could chat with was me! I thought, great, a younger woman wants to talk to me! I am not too long in the tooth then with hay seeds growing out my ears and I have not been consigned to the waste paper basket yet! Okay, Lord please help me, what do I say Lord? She just wanted to talk in confidence, ask questions, and be encouraged in her walk. She wanted to know what would happen if she chose to go ahead. Would I support her? Of course, I said.

And that was the first of many phone calls during which we shared much, personally and spiritually. She grew in leaps and bounds and was finding her way. She has charming children and a great husband, and she really impressed me with her maturity for a younger woman, full of grit and hardworking: a fine role model. The last I heard, her family was settling into a new house and church. She was growing from strength to strength in her relationship with the Lord. We did pray for special protection for herself and her family, as I was aware Satan would do his best to stop the progress! Ultimately, I very much enjoyed helping via the phone, which again was a two-way street as I benefited too.

I have enjoyed Bible study very much. It is important to

*Chapter Eight*

be washed in the word, so to speak, for one's continued spiritual wellbeing. Or, to use another metaphor: think of a soldier putting on his helmet, chest armour, boots, and his fighting equipment, before he goes to battle. We are not only communing with Father, but preparing ourselves for the spiritual battle that goes on in our daily lives as well as the spiritual realm.

Phew! What sort of thriller novel is this? Believe me, the action can be quite horrific and exciting at the same time I have found, and I promise to share some of it with you. Hold onto your hats! (A rollercoaster ride, as I said in the beginning.)

Later, the Lord gave me another scripture from Isaiah: "Others died that you might live; I traded their lives for yours because you are precious to me and honoured, and I love you." When I first came across that scripture it leapt off the page at me. I was going through a difficult time, and did not realize then that Satan's minions were pressing in trying to destroy me, zap my confidence, and split hubby and I up, which had been "normal" for some years.

Around that time, I also saw Satan sneering at me in the form of a visiting family member, a shocking moment, to say the least. Wake up and smell the coffee! I was struggling by myself a wee bit, having to fight for my survival, spiritually and physically. That person was critical of me for signing up for a women's personal development course in makeup and dress, even if it cost $80. I got more than I bargained for, in fact – confidence and a return to self and "get behind me Satan." This visitor thought $80 was an unreasonable cost, and said as much; their malicious intent was evident on their face. But I dealt with it with my own optimism and the fortitude of Jesus. Amen! Thank you Lord.

# Chapter 9

Ongoing battles over the years were still quite vicious, but they have been mostly stopped, except for a few flare-ups here and there. Have I stood down? Never in your life, there is too much to lose. With the Father's help, I keep my head above water! In fact, all of me; is above water, in His hands!

So all my Christian life I have been walking in the Holy Spirit River (another reference to the Old Testament). Jesus has appeared to me on numerous occasions, you just can't beat that, it has been really wonderful.

What I could do without, is Satan attacking me before, during or after the task the Holy Spirit calls me to do. Satan resents good things happening and is always seeking to destroy if possible the works of the Holy Spirit. I just get on with the task fighting my way through the cesspool to victory.

Funnily, the attacks often come (*wham*, the blow!) through my husband, as I am most susceptible to him. I am a strong person, but not perfect and as I said, the one person in my life who means everything to me; is able to hurt me for those very reason's, even if it is unwittingly not deliberate, but orchestrated by Satan. My Bloodhound nose, sniffing out its "prey" (Satan) skills, just desert me and evaporate into thin air and I don't see the "wood from the trees" and I am convinced that hubby is negative towards the work of the Lord and my part! I swallow it; hook, line and sinker most times!

The best I can explain is that a spider web woven to catch its prey is intricate and tangles its victims.

The truth of the matter is that there is no problem at all, just Satan stirring and men being men! So being a woman and "perfect" I complain, mistake number two; the first being an idiot and blind. And is hubby pleased, when I've said, "hey mate," definitely not! Have you heard of grovelling...? I can just picture the man lapping up the cream after this confession!

Eve's story of being deceived in the Garden of Eden by the Serpent stands out right now! Gee, thank you Jesus for reminding me of that one!

Nasty attacks or mind games by Satan (perpetrated through other people I encounter in my life) make up a part of this story. And there are many ways in which such attacks can manifest. I recall a story told to me by a Portuguese missionary friend some years ago now. One night, while walking home, to her horror she spotted some demon spirits enter an animal which then tried to attack her, but of course she used the authority of Jesus to bind them in His name and claimed the blood of Jesus to cover her and protect her from harm. Her story has stayed with me, and I think of it often when undergoing similar assaults.

I always bind Satan myself when necessary, but sometimes I am slow to do that when I am not on top of things sometimes, for one reason or another. I rely on the power of prayer – made even more powerful when done with two or three other Christians together in prayer; spiritual warriors on the same side of the battle. It is very easy to believe Satan's lies

*Chapter Nine*

or lose sight of what is actually happening; such are the wiles of Satan and his often subtle traps. Father says he's roaming round like a roaring lion in search of dinner, eager to devour us. But praise God, He is there and in control; Amen. Early on I gained a couple of lessons about this myself.

Meanwhile, there is an ongoing battle against darkness that we are called upon to fight, like in the Old Testament again, when an angel had to fight for 21 days before another angel came to his aid, allowing the first angel to break through the satanic realm in order for a prayer to be answered, for the recipient. We are required to pray to aid the movement of the Holy Spirit, because that is the way The Father has allowed it to be; for a certain length of time while Satan reigns over the earth. This is where the Father has had me serve a bit.

Another time when I helped my brother Denny was when I was concerned for his predicament, that being, he was finding it difficult to follow the path, the Lord had laid out for him; so I was praying for him with this in mind as Satan was trying to stop Denny following that path, with some pretty vicious attacks.

While praying one day, suddenly I felt the urgency to pray in tongues and then I heard the words, *"it is over"* and the urgency to pray disappeared. This was news! I had a message from Dad for Denny; Great! "Whoopee," I hear down the phone line. Again later, I find out he had been hanging on by his fingertips spiritually because of a battle raging all around him. Denny starts to move on following the Lords path and Wham! He's on the phone asking for some help to win the battle he's in the thick of right then! This is the attack he related to me.

He suddenly felt dizzy, went blind, a splitting headache coming out of nowhere and just about had him falling down, only saving himself, with gripping the truck right behind him! He thought he was going to pass out and did! When he came round he was still holding on to the truck door that was open wide. Had he not been holding on he would have fallen onto the road and been run over! With pinhead vision then, feeling real bad, a nightmare drive home ensued; passing out again when he had made it home!

Denny said it felt like he had been poisoned! With prayer, we overcame Satan.

Another spiritual battle in my early 30's came when I had to hire my own home help and I did not realize she was interested in cult matters and wanted to go to the "Spiritualist" church! For those of you who don't know, that is Satan's church. I politely dismissed her and thought all would be well, but later that night, hubby was asleep and I awoke to a black thing there, OH... The heart skips a beat! So, straight away I starting praying, asking the Holy Spirit to come. I bound Satan I think!

It was a terrifying but a helpful introduction to "spiritual warfare." I must confess, the next day I went round anointing the doors with oil. *Shaken but not stirred!* Hubby was convinced I was weird, as these things were foreign to him. Now he just thinks I am passionate about Jesus. So we have been upgraded!

Join the club. It is a life changing experience. Take up the challenge and find Jesus and dare to grow in Him, you will not be disappointed ever in Jesus, Holy Spirit or Father.

*Chapter Nine*

Here's another example of answers to prayers I have had. A simple one is I remember asking the Father to stretch my food so I could feed the family. Sure enough, it came to pass, and it was the saving grace we had needed as finances were tight.

Another time, we were struggling to find a house in our price range. At that time I received an amount from ACC related to my RSI (Repetitive Strain Injury), and I asked the local minister, who needed help, so that I could help with money. When he suggested who would be a good recipient for the money, I handed over a cheque for the tithe portion of the amount I had received, and the rest went to a much needed dishwasher. What happened after I had tithed that money was we found a house that was in better condition than we could afford and just scraped into the three bedrooms badly needed (as our budget was for two bedrooms) and close by were two good schools. We also bought in a better area as well. Thank you Lord.

# Chapter 10

Allow me to return to the story of my cosmetic surgery. Unfortunately, afterward, I went downhill quickly and was unable to even walk. Hubby dialled the ambulance and I went to hospital, where it was discovered that I had a clot the full length of the main artery in my left leg! They rushed to save me. The A&E doctor was excellent, but the ward experience was miserable!

I left hospital in a fragile state. They had arranged a local doctor to look after me. That turned out to be a comedy of errors! No joke at all; there was some "sort of" system failure and the local doctor was not available to look after me and we were left up in the air with no alternatives; continuing to fall through the cracks in the system. A nightmare, that just got worse. So we were on our own again, hours away from our own doctor in Christchurch, whom we trusted! We got more help from him down a phone line, than on the spot help from the local medical bods! I was put onto Warfarin in hospital for six months with the expectation that it would hopefully aid the clot to dissolve itself. That was the medical treatment available for clots: I was also told the clot could break off at any time and I would die instantly. The other alternative was bleeding to death! I could not walk very well and had crutches and swelling in both legs.

As a result of continual infections in the calf wound of my left leg. I was told that I could have no other medications for any more infections, so I went to the chemist to see if I could help myself and came home with Manakau Honey and eventually when I got back to the cosmetic surgeon, he told us that, it was the honey that had bought the stitch to the surface. The doctor who missed the stitch remaining in my leg wound also told me a sore on my forehead was nothing to worry about.

A few months later, hubby shifted us to Hokitika for a new job, which would save 45 minutes of travelling time one way. Inside six months of coming off the warfarin, which thins the blood to help the blood to circulate, as clots act as blockages; the first clot had dissolved from the top of the leg, as far as the knee, but I got another clot as long as the first one!

This time, the A&E doctor was the same one I had seen previously and he was really angry to hear my case had "fallen through the cracks." So he looked after me until I was well enough to travel to go back to the Christchurch GP "to get looked after properly!" Also I was back on warfarin for life, with the same possible consequences as above. The A & E doctor told me to learn to manage the warfarin myself, as I would last better if I did.

At this stage we had to stop every half hour while driving for a walk, when we were travelling to Christchurch. Over those Southern Alps again! *Ping pong time!*

Anyway I was glad to see the old doctor again, I can tell you!

I was stunned and distressed to find out from another

*Chapter Ten*

Christchurch specialist that dying was a real possibility. As my old doctor had explained to me, I was at less risk of more clots, and dying if they did not try to dissolve this clot, as it was far more dangerous to try. It rather felt like I was cast in the lead role of a Shakespearean tragedy! I have called it "The rabbit in the headlights." (Spotlight)

It was the midnight hour, when all is black and quiet and quite creepy, being wet and rainy and windy, and moving shadows everywhere, on the edge of Kumara (pronounced like car-maara). There is bush everywhere, you can barely see. It is an old gold mining town originally. And there, I was weaving and wobbling down the road, by a graveyard; it sure felt like it, to stretch the legs and to try and stop the body fizzing and driving me insane with lack of circulation, in the glare of the car headlights with hubby watching over me all comfy and warm in the car in contrast to outside it; mind you he was exhausted his self! I had felt trapped in the car, my body screaming in agony as I struggled to control the shrieking fizzing, that also had arrived in my mind too; bordering on losing it. I was dragging my heels to get back in the car because the agony was beyond endurance. Eventually I climbed back into the car and we left Kumara behind, forging ahead into the pitch black of the night, wind howling and buffeting the car as we made our way onto the coastal road to home. Home: a sight for sore eyes!

I found out later that trips like; such lengthy coast to coast trips (500 km return) in one day were out! "You now have to stay overnight, the body can't handle it!" Really! We were also told then there would be no running, or jumping or any physical activity that might break off a piece of the clot, which

*The Jesus Experience*

would kill me instantly. In any event, at that stage, even walking was difficult, I had a pair of crutches and on top of that I couldn't bend my knee back without yelling my head off in agony. I could not even stand in one place more than a minute at that stage!

Ten years later I occasionally do a day trip, but it is still extremely difficult to deal with the corresponding problems. We are always stopping and going "walkies." Also, I have to find somewhere to sit with my legs up for a minimum of thirty minutes! In recent years I have had to travel to Oamaru with hubby a few times, a full six hours of driving, one way, not including the stops! We would take the shortest route through the mountains, which meant, the four wheel drive road off the top of Porters Pass, through the high country and down another zigzag right onto the Rakaia Gorge bridge, where we would stop, for a while, as there were benches for my legs as well as taking in the fantastic view in the high country of the very wide and long river high in the mountains!

The picnic stop is at the end of a high bridge across the gorge itself; the zigzag gravel road we took on this route drops us down onto, literally, the foot of the bridge and the main highway again. From there the gorge disappears from sight due to the closing in of the mountains, and the picnic spot looks down river going towards the east coast, which you cannot see. The senses just revel in the invigorating fresh air and the majestic grandeur of the sweeping vista looking down the river.

Further down south there's the braided Waitaki River and another bench for the legs! Again another fantastic stop, this time situated on the banks of the river itself, rushing and swirling, goggling by on its way to the sea. We are not far from

*Chapter Ten*

the ocean here and the view is equally marvellous. Looking west into the distant background, the mountains regally display their dazzle of colours: lilac, blue and grey. We are surrounded by pine trees, whose shade cools the area around the bench on which we sit, on a hot summer's day. From the bench, the water happily sings along its way, backed with the chorus of the cool breeze winging its way through the trees and the gentle flutter of the birds wings. It is a charming place to stop. By now we know every bench there is to sit on, like a dog knows every lamppost!

So the mode and the ability of travel changed drastically from what we were used to! For example one weekend to get away from the DIY (do it yourself home improvements), we hopped in the car and headed south. Lunch was at Tekapo, about three hours away; afternoon tea was at the bath house cafe on Queenstown's lakes beach front, where we watched The Earnslaw, an old steam ship of about a hundred years old, coming full steam up lake towards us, literally in your face. It is something really worth seeing. Then we carried onto Invercargill at the very bottom of the south island, some nine hours away from Christchurch, where we dined on fish and chips with friends there – all this in a day's drive! The following day, we drove all the way back to Christchurch.

# Chapter 11

We shall now sail forth, into the hurricane of the next road trip – the belly of the beast!

On this trip to my Christchurch doctor, I had to drive myself; hubby just could not get any more time off work. We were living in Hokitika by then, farther south down the coast. Hokitika is a wee seaside tourist town nestled into a wide valley running from the sea to the Alps, with the river bordering one side of the town. The town is surrounded by farming and the beautiful Hokitika Gorge, as well as a thick tangle of bush. The shopping area is bordered by the river and the sea, a pleasant stroll at any time; the streets are all very wide and open, plenty of space, giving a light, airy quality to the town.

Before departing, I was reluctant to go at all as it was a pretty big deal with the clot, and travelling alone was not advisable! But I had no one else to take me. The other daunting prospect was trying to drive with the RSI (repetitive strain injury, now known as OOS), an ailment with which I could barely cope, even with painkillers. Even short trips into town were a challenge. I also had to drive in gloves with a steel insert in them, to keep the wrists straight, also I have to keep my arms resting right up against me and hold the steering wheel at the bottom only as the arms just could not bear the pain if you lifted them up. Believe me, the pain has been that bad over my life, I just wanted to go to hospital and ask them to put me to sleep until the pain went away. I also knew it would take a while for my head to clear when I arrived, so as not to sound like a burbling idiot and to be able to cope! Staying overnight was also a necessity. I was worried about looking after myself as well.

Nevertheless, I decide to make the trip, and with the aid of painkillers and my own determination, I left home. But just before the town limits, I nearly turned back! At that moment, the RSI, starting screaming at me and I'm thinking; "What? I haven't done anything yet!" It simply did not register with me then that it was the second attempt to stop me in my tracks!

And a couple of seconds later, this black cloud appeared out of nowhere suddenly. What the? The black cloud was hovering! It did not click then, what it was and what was happening, not till way down the road! Suddenly, I felt like I was fighting a hazy, dull mind and finding it difficult to think! Amidst the duress of this mental haze, which was pressing in from all sides I took a long deep breath, thinking I have to get to Christchurch and I must stop for a walk shortly. That hazy, dull mind just did not go away. The black cloud presence looked just like a charcoal black thunder rain cloud, solid fog like with whispery bits, flying along the side of the car. That was all I saw then, not knowing, there was more to come or that I was the target under spiritual attack. (That black cloud was actually a demon.)

I continued on my way. Several hours, I was rounding a blind bend (the so-called "Death's Corner") when without warning a great big dirty tandem truck appeared in front of me, moving at a crawl, and I was about to rear end it, with nowhere to pull over, a steep drop off the side of the road, and only seconds to make a decision.

My other choice was to pass if I had enough engine power to do so and of course if the road was clear on the other side. I gripped the steering wheel and decided to move out and get past the truck before it was too late. There were no other vehicles and as I pulled out to pass the truck, the black cloud presence instantly vaporised. *Poof!*

But even as I snapped out of the haze, more drama rose up before me. Oh...help, please Father! There before my eyes, (sticking out like stalks?) was a vehicle, where there had been no vehicle before, barrelling straight toward me! My foot is down and I am in the motion of passing the truck. The truck starts inching its way left slightly, which allows me to just scrape by and miss the approaching vehicle by a couple of inches, give or take. I am onto the viaduct. The truck is fine, I see in the rear view mirror, and so is the other vehicle (which was going too fast for this road anyway) in order to be able to get round "Death's Corner" instead of over the side of it.

Even scarier, I am sure that that vehicle was not there when I pulled out to pass the truck. Hair on the back the neck standing up stuff! The black presence did not come back, thank goodness, and it was then that I realised I had been under spiritual attack right from the very beginning. It was a miracle that nobody was killed or hurt!

Ominously, when the black cloud departed, in the cloud appeared the vague shape of an evil-looking, snarling face. Ephesians 6:12 (RSV), "For we are not contending against flesh and blood, but against the principalities, against the powers,

*The Jesus Experience*

against the world rulers of this present darkness, against the spiritual hosts of wickedness in the heavenly places."

I survived the belly of the beast with the help of the Lord. I did not see any angels of the Fathers, but that does not mean there weren't any, at all. I was a bit busy at the time! I can bet my bottom dollar that I had nothing to do with the result. Father must have had someone praying (interceding) for me, as well as Jesus himself; otherwise, the outcome could have been catastrophic.

The route to Arthur's Pass village was downhill and twisting like a slalom (ski run), but first another short steep climb awaited me – the steepest on the whole road, then the slope made even more hazardous by the possibility of falling rocks.

The village is little more than a cafe with a petrol pump, the Department of Conservation office (DoC), railway station, a policeman and holiday shacks in the middle of nowhere, it was the only place I could stop by myself for safety's sake, and headed for the café. Then I still had left to drive the narrows, the cliffs, the lakes, four high country stations, Porter's Pass, and a ford or two. After I saw the bottom of Porter's Pass five hours later, I still had to skirt the last mountain, Conrad straight, and then over the plains past the agricultural zones of Springfield and Sheffield, which passed in the blink of an eye. Later there's still the city to cross, to get to the doctors, but first I stopped at Darfield, at a cafe with a clock tower and garden centre, to gather myself and rest some more before the final assault over the plains and to the city of traffic lights and one way streets! That was some drive!

At the doctor's, the penny dropped! Bang! Satan had been trying to kill me or ensure that I would not reach my Christchurch

## Chapter Eleven

doctor because then the unhealed sore on my forehead, would be revealed as cancerous and the immediate surgery that was necessary. I was somewhat taken by surprise at the turn of events! I hoped the cancer had not already entered the blood stream. Then it would have been all over, over.

My point being I did not know I had a problem in the first place. I was going back to my old doc, after some time, on the suggestion of the A&E doc; till there was a doc closer at hand that could give me the proper medical attention I needed. This visit was to check on me re the warfarin medication; with the doc I could trust to look after me.

As a consequence of the doc noticing the unhealed sore (with his eagle eyes!) by pure chance; as we were chatting and in shaking my head, he noticed the sore and straight away said that's cancerous. What? Out comes the miners helmet light and an extra inspection, he questions me to find out, that I had already asked about it and had been told it was fine! Mistake! Result: I am sent away with a note to take to the cosmetic surgeon who was expecting me just for a check; next.

I arrived in the nick of time for the appointment with the cosmetic surgeon, but once he was informed of my situation, I was quickly scheduled for another procedure; the removal of the unhealed sore on my forehead; then and there! That night, staring into the mirror of the hotel room where I booked a night's stay, I was not a pretty sight. The blood was seeping through the bandage as if I had been beaten up, as some fellow guests commented. They did not know the half of it of course and I didn't enlighten them either!

Well that was the end of that day's nightmare journey. I just had to do the return trip again the next day! How lucky

*The Jesus Experience*

could a girl get! Another trip the next morning back to the cosmetic surgeon!

I headed for home again and a week later was relieved to learn that the cancer had not entered the blood stream! Hallelujah!

It was time to count my blessings. But also time to reflect on the "Satanic attacks" that had produced this strange sequence of events:

- Hubby not being able to take time off work
- The sudden flare-up of the RSI, for no apparent reason just as I left home
- The sudden appearance of the black cloud presence (a demonic force)
- The incident in the gorge orchestrated by the black demonic force.
- The cancerous mole concealment.

How was the help I desperately needed during that incident in the gorge delivered to me? I can only assume Jesus compelled another Christian to pray and wage war on my behalf. We are told our praying is vital for releasing the freedom of the Holy Spirit's work here on earth and also for allowing the Father's angels to overcome the demonic forces in order to come and help us. As I have already said, Satan is allowed to rule this world for now. That is my understanding of these things.

Or, consider this recent example. One night, in my sleep, I heard my name being called over and over with some urgency, waking me up alert, aware of the need to pray in tongues,

## Chapter Eleven

which I proceeded to do, until the urgency receded. Who was calling me? I believe it was Father calling me by name, as in the story of Samuel in the Old Testament, since it was Father who reminded me about Samuel as soon as I woke up, assuring me it was Him. I have no idea what I was praying about, even now; I just heard and obeyed. I mentioned this to my brother as this was the first time I had heard Fathers voice calling me when I was asleep, literally calling me, Wendy, Wendy, Wendy and he said "of course it was from above!" Denny meant it was Father calling and as he was in a Public place, surrounded by people, when I rang, so he phrased his reply that way. To the uninitiated it would sound crazy, but let me assure you I am not crazy and that was, Father communicating with me as someone else had a need of help; just like I did.

But Satan would prefer people to think that there is no God, that Jesus is not the Son of God and could not possibly save them, and instead have them looking for answers to life and eternity with spiritualist mediums (Satan's helpers in that occult stuff). Satan would have people believing in anything like humanism or doing drugs etc; as long as it keeps people away from knowing Jesus, personally as their saviour.

The battle of Good against Evil rages on in all forms and levels, that is; spiritually, physically and mentally. The battle will end when Father calls the time as He says in the Bible. In the meantime the Gospel of Jesus Christ is to be shared everywhere, so that every person gets to hear it and that they have the freedom to choose to accept Jesus into their lives, thereby becoming children of God, or not.

# Chapter 12

**HERNIA:** The next pieces in the jig saw puzzle is a rare hernia and two further small clots in the already compromised leg, right behind the left knee. By this time hubby had shifted us back to Runanga. The hernia happened a couple of years after the move.

At first, I didn't even know that I had a problem! The tummy button had changed a little and I assumed it was to do with the body ageing. So, I didn't worry about it and just mentioned it to the local doctor (a good one) in passing that it had been like it for a while. Without hesitation, the doc informed me 'it is a hernia and off to hospital you shall go!'

I was assigned to a surgeon from the States, who informed me he didn't want to do the operation but he would have to, as if he didn't, I would die and it had been a while (not good) and if he did it there was a 70% chance of my dying. I don't remember why he said he didn't want to do the operation; I remember being stunned, shocked and a comment about my weight. Unfortunately I did not have hubby with me; having no hint of what was to come.

I remembered the bottom line though and that was; even if I survived the op, he was worried about me getting a bug that would kill me.

Ultimately, I underwent the op successfully and got to go home briefly. But sure enough, I was infected with the bug and earned another trip back to the surgical ward – and isolation! I was loaded up with antibiotics. Next the surgeon did a bit of bush surgery! That is meant kindly, as he delved into my stomach, hand and arm disappearing into my insides to cut something! I felt it! It was like someone casually rustling round in a tool box, except it was me!

I can only imagine what it is like for soldiers on the battle field. I remember saying to Tonto (house resident) "that will be a $2 charge for the privilege of that experience, thanks," which elicited a grin and made me feel better! I told the house resident a few days later that I had nicknamed them both after that experience for a laugh; as Tonto and the Lone Ranger. He grins and says to me which character was he, Tonto or the Lone Ranger, suggesting it was the Lone Ranger of course! And I had reserved the latter for the surgeon! *Whoops!*

The surgeon informed me that the thing that had saved me was that… wait for it… *"I was large."* If not for that, I would be dead! (In fact the surgeon had in the beginning told me off for being big.)

Nevertheless, I am alive. The surgeon did his job, much appreciated of course, and the Father, in whose hands my fate rested, let me live to see another day. It was not my time to die, by His grace.

Recovery, however, took a long time. Years passed before I could even carry my own washing basket to the outside line, and two years to get back to the gardening. It also took about six months give or take to be able to carry a loaf of bread, a litre milk, six apples in a shopping bag!

*Chapter Twelve*

I was given home help for quite a while, which made a big difference. I have found with taking the warfarin medication (blood thinner) it prolongs the healing process and that was confirmed much later by a professional. In my case it was three years before I was completely better and able to do things without the objections of my weary body. A simple scratch from a rose for example takes a week to seal up again and can bleed at a drop of a hat, a consequence of taking warfarin; a gentle knock will bruise badly.

Recovering from the Hernia, was a bit like being stopped in a traffic queue, right under a waterfall's thundering deluge waiting on the road works to be completed (my healing) and for my turn to go, impatiently tapping the fingers on the steering wheel, thinking "hurry up, guys; I have things to do and places to go, (back to normality and independence)!" Or I could just explain it by saying; waiting forever in a checkout queue, till it's your turn!

In any case, I am just recounting the hernia recovery story for your entertainment. That's all folks! (Yeah right, don't give up your day job Wendy!) Thank you Lord.

**DAILY LIVING:** As you may have surmised, daily living became difficult with the onset of the RSI some three decades ago. I have endured periods of just sitting in a chair staring at the walls, being fed and dressed since I was unable to do such daily, simple tasks until the pain subsided. The RSI has forced me to live on pain killers, rely on the relief of massages and, later, natural products, which have made a huge difference and gave me back a limited amount of life and freedom. But still, these gains can be snatched back again rather violently.

So life goes up and down depending on the level of pain. Each onset of complications leaves me again unable to walk or look after myself, let alone tend to the house work, garden or the tramping. Then things are suddenly better and like an old steam train, off I go again, till the next station. Imagine the train: it is stoked and getting up a head of steam and the running till an incline appears and it slows down drastically and becomes puffing billy, slowly chugging and grunting up the hill, the wheels spitting sparks, determined to get to the station before all the steam disappears and the dampers are just left to slowly glow, waiting to be stoked again. And the motto is "I think I can, I think I can." I *know* I can. Praise Jesus.

The positive spin on this is that I have had the time to listen to the Lord and learn a lot and do other things that would not have been possible otherwise, like the volunteer work and the prayer. Also, I was always there to spend time with the children. Later, hubby sold the motels and got a job, and I carried on doing whatever I could when and how I could.

One thing I am dying to be able to do is walk the Spring Creek track, which meanders through railroad tunnels and along a tall gorge. Alongside runs a river with its gentle sounds amongst the tall majestic bushclad mountains surrounding the trail; underneath a strip of blue sky too high to touch. The mood of the canyon walls lining the river is one of mellow graciousness, established solid dignity, carved through timeless ages, melding their character together with dappled flickering light, sensing a Royal Holy Presence; just waiting, beckoning my return, to enchant me once more with their warm welcome.

And yes, my gardening will be severely adjusted (it was sheer

## Chapter Twelve

hell before, but I enjoy it) so I can at least manage the vegetables with hubby's help digging the garden. I am looking forward to being on a new committee and being able to drive myself to and from errands, even to helping collect wood from the forest. Okay going to a show will remain mighty difficult, but not impossible in a small place! Yes I still have to sit a lot and put my legs up to rest them, that's true, but I did have to do that before amongst many other things of daily life requiring adjustment, reconfiguring or plain not at all. But it is nothing short of a miracle to be typing this! (With my arms hanging down like a monkey!) Even things like ironing are a challenge: I only iron one garment on a rare occasion as this is murderous agony.

One example of sheer determination and stupidity was when we first shifted back to Runanga, where we live now. Hubby's back was pretty sore and the house had to be painted. He persevered with the roof and then I put on my gloves with steel bands, took some pain killing pills and set to work on painting the house. But it was excruciating! To try and stop some of the escalation of the pain, hubby would push hard on all the sore parts for as long as I could stand it, yelling all the time! Anybody hearing that would have thought hubby was murdering me! We got it done; I made a point of it, though yes, I was useless again for a while!

So, what are we up to? Yes that's right; another mole off and nearly two years for the skin to join up again after the stitches are out, which happened about a year before the next ailment that befell me, this time involving the knee!

**KNEE CARTILAGE:** As if things couldn't get worse, one day, when I was going down our backdoor steps with the washing basket, the knee cartilage on the good leg ripped – went *ping* just like a violin string breaking and the wave of energy reverberated up and down.

Well on that doorstep I was yelling my head off and didn't even realize I had dropped the washing basket. I couldn't put my foot down for a start, I made the mistake of trying; short lived that was, as I jerked my leg back up into mid air! (I did not know that I had any plans of trying out for a basketball team that day!

With no one around to help me, I managed to drag myself up the step and inside, holding onto the doorways and walls, got myself to the phone and rang the doctor for some crutches. "John can come and collect them" the doctor says, "and come and see me after the weekend" hoping all would be well again. I am moving better now, but some sixteen months later, I haven't recovered totally, although I'm doing some house work and cooking again. Thank you, Jesus.

Well there were many dramas after that, not of my own making. I got to see a surgeon with a little extra help. And on first seeing me, he said "Why are you walking? People with oedema, don't walk, and how long have you been using a stick?" The long and short of it is he did an examination and said you have a tear, there is an operation, but not for you! (1) Result being death. (2) At best more clots, no walking and in a wheel chair for life. We were stunned, hubby and I. He went on to say "If I choose to take the risks, I would need a full resuscitation unit available."

The clots and being on warfarin severely limited my choices. Nevertheless, I was emphatically determined, to do everything in my power to overcome these issues. I got specialist

*Chapter Twelve*

help with what natural products to take to help myself; the rest I left in the Lord's hands. Of course I was not going to have an operation if the risks were so high and I felt no urging and did not hear the Holy Spirit saying go ahead with the operation. So I did not consider it.

When I am better, I am going to see if I can try "my version" of paddle boarding, a very good goal in my opinion. I saw this paddle boarding on telly and it looked super fun, while being exercise too! Basically, I have to get a board, like a surfer's except it has one definite place in which to stand while using a paddle to move about. Well standing for more than ten minutes in one place, I cannot do, my thought is to find something I can lie on and paddle that way on calm lake water. Okay I know it is not likely to be for long, but hey a little is better than nothing.

**DIVERTICULITUS:** this is an issue involving the digestive system and bowel occurring on top of the knee cartilage issue. There was another ambulance ride in the middle of winter to the hospital, with 'right sided' diverticulitis. Oh… so painful. How I got this? I have no idea!

But I was back in hospital again! Maybe I should buy shares in the place! Lord, please what is going on? I would prefer to walk outside with you, in all that majestic scenery that you created; it is really pleasant meandering along a gentle river as it is twinkling by, with a feather of breeze tickling me and the glorious soft dappled light filtering through the trees singing softly, glory to "The Most High God." I am sorry, dear Father it is your will I want, not mine and I know my ways are not yours, thank you.

*The Jesus Experience*

While in hospital, I was told that I was large and yet there were numerous large staff and bigger than me? I was discharged from hospital, unable to shower myself, etc. I was back to being useless again! Seven months later, combined with the knees, I am still hobbled by the diverticulitis and am still restricted to a very limited diet!

I have kept myself amused with the phone, radio, slowly sewing and writing this story. How's that for creativity? But I cannot take the credit as it is Jesus who set the task; this is all for Jesus and the glory of the Father.

My first outing hubby took me on during this time was for the wedding of a really nice young woman we have known since she was little and whose parents are close friends of ours, hence my emphatic insistence on going. It was just before the diverticulitis happened! It was lovely in every way and with very nice people. It was also so good to get out! (A get out of jail free ticket, so to speak, all in good fun! Ouch…! I felt that!) I was really disappointed about not being able to go to the Highland games in Hororata on the Canterbury Plains and after all the effort to go; but upon arrival it was raining and the borrowed wheel chair was not up to the task, in those conditions. The event site was a ruddy great big paddock or two, walking was definitely out! I could see it was not going to work The Highland games (tossing the caber, tug of war etc amongst the clans) are part of Scottish heritage. I had been looking forward to watching the marching bands competitions, like The Edinburgh Tattoo's. Anyway, in February hubby took me to Akaroa to suss out a fishing spot I might manage and we found one to go back to, so that was a bonus and very thoughtful of hubby.

# Chapter 13

**THE BATHROOM:** My Christian brother, he is the one who came to fix up my bathroom in the next story; which actually happened a month before I found myself in hospital again last winter with the diverticulitis. I have saved this story for last as I think it is very special.

We needed a new customized bathroom, since I was unable to use the shub (a cross between a bath and a shower) without my hubby lifting me in and out one leg at a time as I held on to the side for dear life. We hoped to secure a loan to pay for the expensive project but our money was short, until we found a local builder who seemed capable and could do it for a reasonable price. In our ignorance and excitement, we thought the problem would be solved.

This is before even having mentioned it to my brother Denny on the phone. But my brother tells me how wrong we were, in actual fact you barely have enough to buy the materials… Oooh and I am thinking, I have to tell John this bombshell and what the hang are we going to do? Well, before Denny had told us that we were drastically short of the money needed, "you don't have enough for a basic bathroom", he had offered to come down and we said that is lovely, but not necessary, it is a long way and we will be alright, but thank you for caring and offering to come, I wish we could say, "yes please." And we were worried about paying for his expenses on top of paying him for the job. It would not be fair to take advantage, as others had done just that, and we were not going to do that; and what about his work at the steel mill? We did not want to put him in an awkward position at work, as that job was fantastic for him; the Lord had blessed him with it.

A while later Denny rings to say "Dad (Father God) has told me to come and do your bathroom for you. Just pay my petrol and ferry crossings." He would let us know when, as he had some things to do first. Wow! Thank you very much bro; marvellous! Are you sure? "Yes." Father thanks.

It turns out that Denny had days in lieu from his work to use up and would not lose pay either. Thank you Father. So he very generously donated not only his time and skills, but also his lieu days! We will be returning the favour sometime, whenever and whatever that is. Denny wants to build a Christian Retreat when Father tells him to, so I guess we could come in use eventually! It will be our turn to do the trip north to provide unpaid labour!

Denny worked four days in a row doing double shifts at the mill before coming. Driving through the night from Auckland to Wellington, crossing on the ferry first thing in the morning, Wellington to Picton at the top of the South Island, and then a five hour drive, straight through to us.

When he arrived, a mad rush round ensued to obtain the materials needed and were proving elusive! I say that because the new shower had to come all the way from Auckland, since it was out of stock in Greymouth, and it would not arrive to the following week if we were lucky, maybe the day before he

## Chapter Thirteen

was due to go back! It arrived two days before he was going back. We were also short of flooring, nobody in Greymouth seemed to carry any stock, it all had to be ordered and takes time to get here. Another thing to add to the Christchurch shopping list!

Finally, however, things started getting sorted out, thank you Father. The shower came and the flooring was located in town from a left over piece from another job; luckily just the right amount for our bathroom! It also cost considerably less. We got staff prices for most of the stuff needed due to hubby's work. No shopping trip to Christchurch was needed in the end and Denny grins at me and says "notice how things started working out when I turned up!" An angel arrived to save the day;" by special delivery from Father! Praise God. Really bro; that's high powered company you're keeping there!

Gee it was a crazy, frenzied week that one, nothing but bathroom work 24/7. But it was enjoyable at the same time. Denny had bought me a message from Dad too, which had me intrigued to start with, then ensued the conversation and explanation, mighty. So an extra present delivered! Hubby, who was flat out at work, became the "boy" for the week, all hands to the deck; John had taken out most of a wall before Denny arrived under instruction from Denny over the phone! I just basically managed to feed them, with a friend's help providing me with meals. I could not have managed without her help. I don't think Denny starved at our house. I made bacon soup especially for them as I had had the time to do it and guys like meat, and in May it's a good thing to have soup on hand. It took ages to make in different stages as I couldn't stand up long at all! It was very hard that week for me since I was pretty unwell and could barely walk. To go to the Mega store, they both took turns pushing me in the stores wheelchair. We also had to stay in a motel for four nights and just make do after that. We were not turning up to the motel till round 10pm – 11pm and up at 6am; hard yacker (work). Denny was so worried about the work still to do; he left and went back to the house to carry on after we were asleep! We didn't even know he had gone as he was there when we got up!

The following night at the motel hubby got up in the middle of the night and comes rushing back to our bedroom. "Wake up Wendy, Denny's not here and our car is gone!" he said frantically. "Oh! Not much we can do about it, don't worry, he is hardly stealing the car, I hope he is okay." We were a bit worried about him though all the same. It turned out Denny had gone back to the house to carry on with the work.

Then he promptly suggests adding to the work load in getting new lights for the hallway and lounge too since the electrician was already due that day and everything would match and be updated then! At least we should be grateful that it was not adding to his work load! It was a good idea! Talk about a beggar for punishment, the poor guy, no sleep! John had been wondering when and if Denny slept. His tireless work and dedication to the project showed great love for John and I, love that cannot be measured or beaten. It cannot be bought either, and is priceless and freely given. We will be in there batting for him whenever it is necessary, it is nice to know someone has your back covered.

Denny displayed to hubby and I those fine Christ like qualities we all strive to emulate. And as an extra blessing Jesus

*Chapter Thirteen*

was there too with us, actually shining through Denny. And in the blink of an eye, this is what I saw: Jesus himself smiling at me. Taken by surprise, *as Jesus stepped out of Denny!* Whoa there ... stop ... back the bus up! Yes folks, that's right, *Jesus stepped out of Denny*. I could see and feel Jesus' love pouring forth and his humour! His presence surrounded us, and He was enjoying it all, blessing the project and giving me the sense of fun at the carnival. Jesus was projecting this all to me! Jesus had come to say hello to us.

The Father's greatest commandment to us is "to love one another as God loves us" and we are expected to follow it. "Jesus in us is the secret." If we put Jesus first before ourselves, much is achieved for Father's Glory. There is none beside him, He is the Beginning and the End, the Alpha and Omega, the one true God, Father of mankind and creation.

Denny found nothing but problems in the bathroom. They all had to be dealt with: the plumbing, for one, then a new floor, and a lake under the house, new walls, stripping the room back to the frame! So as you have probably guessed he did three weeks' worth of work in one, with hubby's help. Hubby still had the plastering decorating and the clean up to do, when my bro left for home. So hectic does not even describe it. The rubble pile on the driveway was pretty indicative of the frantic action.

After a week of intense labour (including two all-nighters), it was time to say farewell. John drove him to Picton to keep him company and save him some of the driving time as Denny was totally exhausted. It was a Mammoth task. Hubby was a bit strung out as well, which is hardly surprising! He did not tell Denny that in order to drive him, he would have to get the bus to Nelson and stay overnight, then bus back the next day. As for me, I was finally allowed to try the shower out, "very carefully Wendy, so you don't fall etc," only to discover that there was no hot water! Derr! I rang them and got "what woman, you have got it wrong! Did you turn it the right way?" …Yes… five minutes ago, I tried that! Oh! Never mind I'll look when I get home! Thankfully, it turned out to be a simple connection round the wrong way.

My brother tells us the true cost was just over double what we had budgeted! That's some saving and care from Father God. *Thank you Lord*. Did I say Denny discovered a lake under the house as well that he had to fix too! He had hoped the job would be straight forward! He also said the shub would have fallen through the floor before much longer, as the last owners, had stuck a piece of newspaper over the hole, he discovered in the floor with a rock underneath that and they had just installed the shub on top of the hole without repairing the floor!

Though I'm still fragile, I can now shower myself with no help. Can't complain at that! We grinned and bore the chaos for a week in a tiny house with bathroom bits in every room, but what a result! To me that makes my brother a hero and all the time serving the Lord too. We definitely appreciate the love and care that came from my brother and the Lord, our Father.

**BONUS – PLUS:** It is even more of a blessing from the Lord, since my brother found out upon his return, his injuries were severe, knees and shoulder, and that he should have not been able to drive or walk, yet he was, by the grace of "Dad," as he calls Father God. He was indeed walking and working double shifts for the last 18 months and then a road trip from one

*Chapter Thirteen*

island to another involving many hours of driving. If this isn't a miracle and answer to prayer, I don't know what is!

Denny definitely should have his nickname upgraded, don't you think?

My brother was and still is a builder by trade. This is what he has done all his working life, and he's excellent at his craft. You would consider yourself lucky to have found him. But after years of backbreaking labour (often with no one around to help), he damaged himself in the process; his knees need an operation, some of his spine is frozen, and he struggles with pain. He pulled out of the building trade, and managed to get himself a job at the steel mill, which is much easier on his body, but he tells me he was struggling all the same, and it was but for the grace of Dad, that kept him walking when he should not have been. There was some mishap, and he ended up with his shoulder, causing excruciating pain, but again he was able to carry on, for which he was grateful.

Things plodded on and after coming down to help us out, he returned to work, saw a doctor who could not believe how bad he was and was shocked that Denny was working, walking and driving. But he was strong and Dad had made it that way. So in the meantime he had carried on working waiting for another doctor's appointment when all of a sudden at work one day, he became unwell and was unable to continuing working. He was put into a taxi and sent home. At the next doctor's visit, he was told he did not have much of a tendon left, in the shoulder. When they opened him up, it was much worse than they thought! But they performed a repair job, the healing process has begun and he is off work for about six months give or take.

*The Jesus Experience*

So that is why his visit is even more of a miracle folks, as I said above and beyond. Thank you Lord.

There is more! The financial side of things: For John and I, we got a bathroom for half the actual cost it should have been and also to even get that tiny loan. Denny said as soon as he said he was coming, his things started working out too! For one, he had enough days in lieu to use for the trip and this meant his wage was still intact and some other things suddenly started working out for him, after he said he was coming too. So we both got a finance miracle each. Thank you Dad very much.

# Chapter 14

From Denny's perspective: this is how the bathroom story affects him.

Denny says the bathroom renovation was a respite from struggling with a spiritual battle he has been deeply into. He relates it as a 'Wilderness' experience, where he is totally reliant on Father God, fighting his way out of the jungle slaying dragons, with close encounters with his life at risk; while growing closer to Jesus.

It is a hard place to be at times, on the frontline of the battle between Heaven and Hell. Denny can verify that Hell exists from a "flying" visit there and of course we know Heaven is real because God is real; He gave us Jesus, along with supernatural miracles. Denny has also had a flying visit to heaven.

In the bible there is the story of Daniel in the Lion's Den; he remains unharmed and then there were those three men of God who were thrown into the furnace, but remained untouched by the fire. Evil had tried to destroy them and failed, because the men were in the Fathers care.

This was Denny's position, when "Dad"(Father God) told him to go south; likening it to; just lifting him up out of the dross and popping him down away from the battle for awhile.

Denny's favourite place of rest and peace; as "Dad" gave it to him; is his shack in the North. (More of a tin shed really.)

Now the Holy Spirit had been speaking to Denny about the 'Job' scripture "I will return all that is lost to you." That meant specifically brother and sister being reacquainted and giving him another brother John (hubby). There is more to it of course but that's for another story. The very first fruition of that promise for Denny, from the book of Job; was that Father God telling Denny to call Him "Dad."

The Holy Spirit also told Denny that his trip south was tied into some other plans of Father's for Denny (to be explained at a future date), but obedience was critical so that they could come to fruition; so he would not miss the boat so to speak!

Two plans of the Fathers came to fruition with Denny's trip here; one was to deliver a special message from Dad to me (private). Also there was the opportunity of having fellowship together, hubby, Denny and I, establishing a solid base to build upon, for future plans of Fathers. This was also when the seed was planted for this book and our collaboration on it and in our spiritual lives too. Denny has been told there are more books to write and what they are to be. As I said there's more in the pipeline from Father.

As Denny pointed out his trip here in obedience to Father, is producing all sorts of results and to our benefit as Dad loves us.

In faith, acceptance and believing Fathers word, Denny followed Fathers instruction and thereby bringing about Fathers Divine Will to happen definitely and the Holy Spirits hands are untied to make it happen.

It is most important to believe when Father God speaks; "as God cannot lie." If we did not believe/doubted that; well we rob ourselves of Fathers will happening. So this is why Denny stepped out in faith to come south and we were blessed with Jesus' visit during the bathroom project and since.

As to the Christians 'wilderness/desert' experiences, in our walk with Jesus, we can be there for any number of reasons, such as; to be closer to Father, to grow more in His ways, protected, un-repented sin, unbelief, disobedience, an attention getter, deliverance. To discover why, we just need to get closer to Father and His word (Bible), and ask Him and wait patiently for His response. While waiting, we remember that His ways, thoughts or timing are not like ours and we must always love, trust, praise and thank Him and keep walking in His ways; realising that Father is in control of everything. Also Jesus reminded us to address Father with our prayers in Jesus' name.

But let me describe to you the vision I saw. It was of Jesus sitting, waiting on Mt Searle. I did not know what this meant at the time, but my brother interpreted it for me. He said it was of Jesus waiting on a local spiritual battle against Satan, to be won. Also Jesus was waiting for people to ask Him back into their churches instead of Satan. This experience highlights the critical need for prayer against the demonic forces. But in the interest of privacy, that's all I can say now. This is very much our experience:

"I will not die but live, and will proclaim what the Lord, has done." Psalm 118:17 (NIV)

**MIRACLES:** This is a story of Jesus, the "Living Miracle of Grace," who fills these pages at every turn. May you too see Jesus and feel His love.

John 11:40 (TLB) "But didn't I tell you that you will see a wonderful miracle from God if you believe?" Jesus asked her. (Jesus was speaking to Martha about her brother Lazarus at his grave; before Jesus spoke to Father and called to Lazarus to come forth from his grave; no longer dead, but alive.)

John 11:47,48 (TLB) "For this man [Jesus] certainly does miracles. If we let him alone the whole nation will follow him". (The Bible is full of miracles, displaying Fathers Supernatural Power and Sovereignty and His love for us.)

Colossians 1:27 (TLB) "And this is the secret: that Christ (Jesus) in your hearts is your only hope of glory."

**VISIONS:** Visions are a form of communication from Father God. I have quoted below a passage from a very public Christian minister's book, *How to Interpret Dreams and Visions* by Perry Stone, from which I gained a great deal.

> 'Open visions' occur when the visionary is fully alert, awake, and aware of his physical surroundings.
> All men, women, and children are tripartite beings, consisting of a body, soul, and spirit. Dreams seem to emerge or develop more in the realm of the soul, whereas visions are deeper manifestations, which are conceived within the spirit of the person.
> *A vision* always concerns the future and seldom, if ever, the past, as God's kingdom and human life always move

*Chapter Fourteen*

forward and never look backward. We cannot undo the past, but we can pursue the future. You may spend your entire spiritual walk and never experience a literal night vision while in a deep sleep. However, you must continually live with dreams and visions and desires to be blessed, to be a blessing to others, and to fulfil all that the Lord puts in your heart.

In our lives a *vision* is required to bring about all possibilities and desires in our heart. To build anything, including a home, an office, a business, or a marriage, demands that the participants have some form of vision. The largest things built on Earth began with a mental image in someone's mind. The plan is transferred from the image of the mind to a blueprint on paper, followed by a team of individuals prepared to take the written design and create a visible, three-dimensional object.*

---

\* Perry Stone, *How to Interpret Dreams and Visions*, Charisma House, 2011

# Chapter 15

As to my personal experiences of visions, I have already shared some, but Jesus visited me again standing by my chair reminding me of the bathroom visit and to include it in the story, as I had forgotten all about it! Jesus had a reason for this which became clear from Him further down the track! (Which I will explain shortly.)

First the other vision I have to share is that, I went to a church that the Holy Spirit had impressed upon me to go to. The Spiritual block I had felt previously regarding the church had disappeared and upon entering the church it felt really comfy; and with the sense of I was to be in that church. During the service I saw Jesus arrive up the front of the church, *as a literal Lion* (Jesus is the Lion of Judah) and He was grinning at me with shared amusement, then *Jesus transforms* into the way we are all familiar with seeing Him, still smiling and reminding me of the shared story below. It was funny and yet lovingly shared; while revealing His self to me, as in the book below. And I am grinning like a Cheshire cat.

Now, the shared amusement/joke is that those visions together were also about me having read the book that Jesus also stars in. The true story of Anne Elmer's flying visits with Jesus as "The Lion of Judah" in the book called *Transported* *by the Lion of Judah*, Anne sometimes sat on the Lion's back! And then there was her lying in the hospital bed and asking the Lion (Jesus) laying beside her bed with His eyes shut; saying are you awake? Well the Lion's eyes open and there's a comical look on His face and he replies with; "yes, I am always awake" …humorously spoken!*

So that is why the three visions went together, even though each of them, were in different circumstances. Wow, pretty awesome!

I'll slip in here with a "tongue in cheek" jest for Jesus, folks. You see I thought I would be funny with Jesus and I started writing on my pad and the next thing I know is that *Jesus* is *peering* over my shoulder laughing to see what I was writing! Jesus was joining in on the fun with me. Wow. I grin and Jesus is gone and I carry on.

My little quip was that Jesus I have loved doing this book, but I left my sewing to do it, not that that's a problem, it's just that I need some decent winter clothes and winter is nearly here; so could I please *fit* in some sewing? But I don't want to miss out on anything else with you please.

> If you will humble yourselves under the mighty hand of God, in His good time He will lift you up.
> Let Him have all your worries and cares, for He is always thinking of you and watching everything that concerns you.

---

\*   Anne Almer, *Transported by the Lion of Judah*, Elijah List Publications

*Chapter Fifteen*

Be careful – watch out for attacks from Satan, your great enemy. He prowls around like a hungry, roaring lion, looking for some victim to tear apart.

Stand firm when he attacks. Trust the Lord; and remember that other Christians all around the world are going through these sufferings too.

After you have suffered a little while, our God, who is full of kindness through Christ, will give you His eternal glory. He personally will come and pick you up, and set you firmly in place, and make you stronger than ever. (1 Peter 5:6-10)

**FINALLY:** There is another marvellous, wonderful, joyful, ecstatic experience I have to tell you about, and it is ongoing! The Holy Spirit has been nudging me along and directing me on this story as you already know, but what you don't know is that there is also someone else: my "spiritual cheerleader." Yes that's right folks, *Jesus* himself has *visited* me. He appeared, full of light and love, with a smile on His face, and His thumb pointing upwards in the recognisable gesture that means "it's okay; the story has My 'seal of approval'. Carry on – thumbs up." *Jesus*, indeed, *has a sense of humour*. His visitations have been indescribably joyful and invaluably encouraging; leaving me with the direction, "This is the way;" follow me into the story, this story is mine and I will show you what goes in it. Also *Jesus says* with a twinkle in His eyes, *this is fun*. His message is projected loud and clear, as *Jesus encourages* me to carry on writing this story.

Jesus has visited a few times now, though the actual number

isn't important. What matters is the life-changing experience of being with Jesus, right beside my chair, adding his own flare to this book, a certain divine "artistic touch." *Wow!* That's right folks, *Jesus came* and *stood* by my chair, *spoke*, telling me what to write, from the very beginning. *Jesus is here in these pages and in person. For real.*

> The light shines in the darkness and the darkness has not overcome it. (John 1:5, RSV)

God bless you all, and I look forward to reading more true life stories/miracles of yours. *Jesus will be thrilled too. (I know!) Jesus is thrilled.*

> If you want favour with both God and man, and a reputation for good judgement and common sense, then trust the Lord completely; don't ever trust yourself. In everything you do, put God first, and he will direct you and crown your efforts with success. (Proverbs 3:5-6)

> I looked in vain for anyone who would build again the wall of righteousness that guards the land, who could stand in the gap and defend you from my attacks, but I found not one. (Ezekiel 22:30)

The end
...or is it just the beginning?